More Praise for *Leadership Divided*

"Over two millennia ago, Heraclitus observed that 'change alone is unchanging' and 'a man's character is his guardian divinity.' For me, Ron Carucci has compellingly woven these two timeless themes into *Leadership Divided.* The change we face as businesses and as individuals is the constant. Positional authority isn't. We all seem to have the capacity to grow as leaders, but many of us won't. Performance management systems that disproportionately reward individual 'contributions' seem to breed hard-driving idiots. The challenge of creating the right conditions for nurturing the development of leadership is daunting. I found the guidance in *Leadership Divided* to be rich, provocative, and immediately useful. Although it is indeed a challenge to admit that my character, my ability to give, to get, my willingness to be disappointed, my appreciation for the gifts and commitment of others is the foundation of my leadership, I feel confident to do so."

—Tony Siesfeld, Ph.D., partner,
The Monitor Group

"Bravo! In an increasingly global community, this is a must-read for anyone looking to build strong and effective business relationships with those they lead. Carucci provides a veritable blueprint on how to build and leverage these critical relationships to ensure outstanding results. Regardless of a leader's experience level, everyone can benefit significantly from the rich and novel insights in this book."

—Steven Blackman, Ph.D., CEO and publisher,
Metropolis Buenos Aires magazine

"Carucci defines a path for emerging leaders who want to lead in today's competitive global world, but who recognize that the leadership principles and theories left over from yesterday are inadequate for the complexities of tomorrow. A new leadership is called for, or the capable, high-potential leaders in the organization will not step up to fill broader leadership roles. In a marvelous synthesis of conceptual wisdom, down-to-earth application, and insightful, true case stories, Carucci makes the new leadership comprehensible, inspiring, and germane to the world of today. It is a must-read for anyone who is or wants to be a leader for the future."

—Toby Jane Tetenbaum, Ph.D., professor, Fordham University; director, Ed.D., Executive Leadership Program

"Ron Carucci draws you into his book with stories, reflection points, and some well researched positions. Veterans and upcoming leaders alike will benefit from reading and discussing this book. A major leadership transition is looming on our horizon, and though there are plenty of leaders for the next generation, they don't want to lead as they have been led. This book provides a critical framework for a conversation between the generations that will lead the way through inevitable transition."

—Al Erisman, Ph.D., director, Center for Integrity in Business, Seattle Pacific University School of Business and Economics; director, Institute for Business Technology and Ethics; and former director of technology, Boeing Corporation

LEADERSHIP DIVIDED

What Emerging Leaders Need and What You Might Be Missing

Ron A. Carucci

Foreword by Mike Roberts,
president, McDonald's Corporation

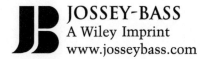

JOSSEY-BASS
A Wiley Imprint
www.josseybass.com

Published by Jossey-Bass
A Wiley Imprint
989 Market Street, San Francisco, CA 94103-1741   www.josseybass.com

Jossey-Bass books and products are available through most bookstores. To contact Jossey-Bass directly call our Customer Care Department within the U.S. at 800-956-7739, outside the U.S. at 317-572-3986, or fax 317-572-4002.

Jossey-Bass also publishes its books in a variety of electronic formats. Some content that appears in print may not be available in electronic books.

Library of Congress Cataloging-in-Publication Data

Carucci, Ron A.
   Leadership divided : what emerging leaders need and what you might be missing / Ron A. Carucci ; foreword by Mike Roberts.
       p. cm.
     Includes bibliographical references.
     ISBN-13: 978-0-7879-8589-9 (alk. paper)
     ISBN-10: 0-7879-8589-9 (alk. paper)
   1. Leadership.   2. Corporate culture.   3. Organizational behavior.   4. Executive ability.   I. Title.
     HD57.7.C3687   2006
     658.4'092-dc22   2006017096

Printed in the United States of America
FIRST EDITION
HB Printing   10 9 8 7 6 5 4 3 2 1

CONTENTS

For Toby

Thank you, from my core, for seeing me, knowing me, and
believing in me.
You have imprinted my life with uncommon love and
wisdom.
You are a champion, mentor, and beloved friend.

FOREWORD

I grew up on the west side of Chicago in a single-parent home. I was blessed with the gift of poverty from a material standpoint, but also blessed with millions of messages that I could be whatever I wanted.

From the earliest age, I can recall being taught that life was about others. I remember standing outside church and watching my grandmother gather with others afterwards. I would hear her ask people, "How are you doing, how are the kids?" or "I haven't seen your husband, is everything all right?" She impressed upon me the importance and power of people and relationships, of participating in the lives of others. She showed me that people can be a source of inspiration and support.

I found those same fundamental lessons to be true of leadership as well. The results we must achieve are an important part of being in business. For McDonald's, they fuel investment in our people, our restaurants, and our brand. But over the years, the most gratifying part of leadership has been seeing people grow and develop into roles that surprised even them. The investment in sharing experiences and personal stories about family and friends, discovering strengths together and shoring up one another's weaknesses, has been the connective tissue that makes being part of a powerful team fun and impacting. It's a key part of striving for excellence. This is never about striving only for an individual's achievement, but about our collective achievement—seeking the good of the whole.

Our organization comprises over a million people worldwide. That's an audacious leadership responsibility. And that includes more than five thousand owner-operators—individual families whose livelihoods and personal capital have been invested in our business. Those relationships drive our decision making and influence our suppliers' and customers' experience of our brand. Our people's relentless drive for performance, as was modeled for us all by our founding leaders such as Fred Turner, is what makes our organization great. And at the core of it all are the relationships—the connective tissue—that creates our common ground. Being in a room full of people who share that common purpose is very exciting. There is no way to describe what it's like being part of a leadership team that is committed to doing the best for the company and our constituents. But we know we have an impact on millions and millions of people. And that matters.

Gone are the days where an enterprise agenda could be owned by a few. If you insist on overly owning the reins of your organization, your potential will be muted. Whether you are a CEO or a department manager, if you don't have your organization aligned around what's important to you and them, there just aren't enough hours in the day, and not enough air in your lungs, to get the job done. Your success will inevitably be limited. You will have thousands of people sitting on the sidelines watching you, not actively engaged in the process of advancing your organization. If relationships are a tertiary, inconsequential part of your leadership, if you operate in an excessively top-down way, I would expect your ability to successfully govern the organization to be short lived. I get very concerned when I meet leaders who believe life is "all about them" or that they have it all figured out. Such leaders inspire me to be even more curious because I know there is always more to be learned and more people from whom I can learn it.

I want to lead an organization where there is a shared understanding among millions about what our purpose is, what we stand for, what our goals are, and what we value. Leadership has got to be a constant source of affirmation and a voice box for the soul of the organization. Issuing dictates without dialogue, conversation, and meaningful exchanges can't work. The globe is too complex, our markets too diverse and evolving, our landscape too dynamic to ever assume a few voices could shape success. That means we need many, many leaders, not just a few.

For us, the markets that consistently outperform others are the ones that have the best relationships between the general managers and the local operators. Time and again I have seen this proven by leaders who exemplify tireless efforts to participate in and build good will with their communities. Around the world, it is clear: when people have a voice and are actively engaged in the business, our performance is good. When that isn't the case, the markets struggle. I would be surprised if that weren't the case for you as well.

I remember a conversation in which Ray Kroc and Fred Turner were meeting with operators, and they were listening very intently. They were curious and wanted to know what was working and what wasn't. They really listened and took to heart what they heard without letting the conversation become personal. That made a huge impression on me.

I will be the first to admit I am far from having mastered leadership. I know I am flawed like any human being. I start my day with the fundamental notion that I can always be better than I was yesterday. There is so much that I don't know. Before I express myself, I try to suspend judgment to see what more I can learn. Sure, I have well-formed opinions about how to run great restaurants and how to enhance our customer experience, but I am always curious to learn more about how we can be better. I take golf lessons. I talk to my wife. I practice my faith. I want my life to read, "How can I make the planet better?" At the end of the day, that's why we are here. There are still days I am impatient. I have to hear painful feedback. But I'm grateful for it. Because it reminds me that there will always be a part of me that can never fully appreciate the chair that I sit in. I have to be reminded that I must go home at night. I'm a father. I'm a husband. I cannot forget who I am. But that doesn't need to quell my desire to effect meaningful and far-reaching change. My west Chicago roots remind me that even I can make a huge difference in the world. And I must be responsible with the influence I have been given to do so.

I loved the movie *Seabiscuit*. When Tom Smith, the horse's trainer, first met Seabiscuit, he said he was a "train wreck. He paced in his stall incessantly. He broke into a lather at the sight of a saddle. He was two hundred pounds underweight and chronically tired. He was so thin, his hips could have made a passable hat rack. And that left foreleg didn't look good." But in the film, Tom looks deeply into Seabiscuit's eyes. And the gaze is returned. Nobody expected that horse to do anything. But Tom saw that "he had spirit." In many ways, I see my job as being like Tom's: to find that look in people's eyes—of strength, yet humility; power, yet vulnerability—and to turn them loose so they can develop and make the organization, and the planet, better.

Seabiscuit's success was born of pain. When the doctor told my wife and me that our daughter had cerebral palsy, and would never be like my other children, I knew how powerless I really was. I felt helpless. I know that vulnerability and hurt—and, ultimately, loss—contribute to leadership in ways I can't articulate. But I know it to be true.

Seabiscuit needed others to realize his greatness. I have had the good fortune of friendships and relationships that have continued to nourish and encourage me, especially in difficult moments. I've needed them to realize any achievements in my life.

And you need others, too.

You need meaningful relationships with those you lead, if you intend to lead well. If you are hoping to prepare your emerging leaders to take the helm of your organization, you can't be estranged from them. And if you are an emerging leader hoping to extend important influence one day, you need, and should want, help from those who have gone before you. It's not at all clichéd to say that divided leaders will fall. In fact, I would say they tend to fall harder these days.

Leadership Divided will help you create those meaningful relationships, if you will suspend judgment and open up to its principles. I've known Ron for years, and I know his passion to build successful organizations and effective leaders. You can trust what you will hear in the pages ahead. As you read, keep your organization and the leaders around you in mind at all times. They are the ones who will ultimately benefit from your time with this book, beyond what you will personally gain.

My best wishes as you govern your organization and search for the greatness in the leaders around you and within yourself. I'm confident the ideas in the pages ahead will help in your pursuit, and my hunch is that you and those with whom you lead will be glad you looked.

July 2006   MIKE ROBERTS
Oak Brook, Illinois   president, McDonald's Corporation

LEADERSHIP DIVIDED

INTRODUCTION

Estuary

There is only one prediction about the future that I feel confident to make. During this period of random and unpredictable change, any organization that distances itself from its employees and refuses to cultivate meaningful relationships with them is destined to fail. Those organizations who will succeed are those that evoke our greatest human capacities—our need to be in good relationships, and our desire to contribute to something beyond ourselves. These qualities . . . are only available in organizations where people feel they are trusted and welcome, and where people know their work matters.

Margaret J. Wheatley, *Finding Our Way*

See if this sounds familiar:

The buzz around the tenth-floor corner office has settled down at the usual 5:30 P.M. in this major corporation's suburban division headquarters. Randy, a seasoned veteran leader with more than twenty years in the organization, is so engrossed in what he is reading that he doesn't even notice his assistant, Lindsey, come in. She drops something on the polished oak credenza, partially to get his attention, and says, "You need anything else before I head out?"

Randy barely glances up, and with a feigned smile he says, "No thanks, Lindsey. Just please make sure Jack knows I want to talk to him tonight before he leaves, OK?"

"Will do," Lindsey replies. "Don't forget to take your talking points for the breakfast with the brand teams tomorrow—I left them right here. Remember it starts at 7:30 A.M. Have a good one."

Randy mumbles, "Thanks, goodnight" as Lindsey leaves. He just can't pull his eyes away from the report he's reading. No matter how many times he stares at the numbers, the picture stays grim. The company's European operations are falling far short of plan for the third quarter, and pressure is mounting to take action. George Henley, the guy responsible for Europe, just isn't cutting it. George has over a decade of experience, and Randy thinks he's a great guy. George had initially seemed perfect for the job, and he'd wanted it for a long time. But now it seemed as if he was just in over his head. Now Randy was going to have to face a difficult conversation with George. And there was an even harder issue to face: just who *could* get this job done?

A loud triple-knock on the door jolts Randy out of his restless contemplation. He looks up to see Jack Leong standing in the doorway. Jack had come to the organization right out of graduate school about nine years back. He had been at the top of his M.B.A. class, and he had enjoyed a series of successful assignments at the company, building a reputation as a real problem solver. Even though Randy liked George a lot, he had come to believe that Jack was the best chance the company had for getting Europe back on track.

"Hey, Jack, c'mon in—thanks for stopping by," Randy said, pushing the reports he had been looking at aside.

"Sure, no problem. What's up?" Jack said, settling into one of the chairs in front of Randy's desk.

Broaching the subject he had in mind suddenly seemed awkward, so Randy said, "Hey, great job, by the way, on the launch last week. I heard fantastic things about the session with the customers, and it sounds like the sales folks are ready to hit the ground running."

Though a sincere compliment, Randy knew that Jack saw right through the skid-greasing intention of the statement. Still, Jack was polite in response, saying, "Thanks, Randy—appreciate your saying so. It really was a team effort."

After about ten minutes and several other weak attempts at golf and sports small talk, Randy finally plowed in, saying, "Look, I won't beat around any bushes here. I want to talk to you about a critical opportunity." Jack was both intrigued and anxious, and he leaned forward attentively.

"You've seen the same data I have on Europe," Randy continued. "It's just not turning around as we'd hoped. George isn't getting the job done, and I'm getting pressure to take action. Our division is the only one exceeding plan overall, and corporate doesn't want to risk the trajectory we're on."

Jack realized the political implications of this conversation, but didn't see the career ramifications for himself. Naïvely, he simply said, "Damn, that's a shame. I thought things were starting to look a little brighter there. Last time I spoke to George he seemed optimistic."

"Well, the data don't suggest any reason for optimism, even if he thinks otherwise," Randy replied. "Look, I know you've got young kids, and your family is really important to you, so I don't present this opportunity lightly to you. But the more I've thought about this, the more I'm convinced you're the one guy we have who could really turn Europe around and get it where it needs to be.

I'd only need you there for two years, maybe three, and I think it could take your career to a whole new place. You have the energy, you're smart and respected around the organization, you know the products and segments better than anyone else around here, and most importantly, I trust you. Bottom line is, I don't think I can afford to wait on this any longer. Obviously I'm not looking for you to give me an answer or even a reaction right now. You need to think about this and talk it over with your wife. Can we talk again in a couple of days?"

Jack struggled not to show how much shock he was in. He was able to stutter out, "Uh, yeah, sure, Randy. Uh, thanks. I'm really overwhelmed, but thanks for the vote of confidence. It sounds like an amazing opportunity for sure. I just need to really think about if it's right for me at this time in my career. But I'll think it over hard, talk with Lisa about it, and I'll get back to you in the next couple of days."

As he shook hands with Randy and walked back to his own office, Jack's mind was a blur. He'd enjoyed the last eighteen months as head of sales and marketing for the division, had finally found his niche, and was very successful at what he was doing. He'd slogged through nearly nine years of hard work and climbing in both operations and marketing. And now, having gotten where he was before walking into Randy's office, he loved his job. And it was clear his people loved him. He'd inherited a mish-mash of disconnected processes and had turned them into a well-oiled machine that was a major factor in the division's successful performance last year. He and his wife, Lisa, had bought a new house just under a year ago, and the kids were in a great school. He was golfing at the club on weekends, he was very involved in his community and his church, and he was happier than ever. Whatever blips were on his future career radar, Randy's offer certainly wasn't one of them.

So, what do you think Jack will do? And more important, besides the substantial personal changes, what are the biggest considerations Jack is weighing as he makes his choice? What do you think will determine whether Randy gets him to take on the challenge?

Our experience tells us that, in very large measure, the last forty or fifty conversations Randy and Jack have had *before* Randy's offer will have lined up most of the things that will influence Jack's response. Contrary to what might appear obvious, simple self-interest is not going to be the only factor in Jack's decision. In fact, for most emerging leaders, self-interest seems to be a criterion of decreasing importance. The quality and depth of Jack's relationship with Randy, how much personal equity Randy has built up with Jack, and Jack's sense of whether Randy is investing in him or using him—these will play a formidable role in how Jack's choice unfolds. The moral of the story is this: if you want to prepare emerging leaders for broader roles in the future of your organization, you must intimately understand what does and doesn't motivate them to consider those opportunities.

CRISIS?

For years now the world has been hearing about the "crisis of leadership" around the globe. Every statistic—from retirement rates and time horizons of baby boomers to shifting values among emerging leaders to the post-Enron-scandal cynical view of anything "corporate"—seems to reinforce one thing: a pervasive belief that we're running short on leaders capable to take the reins of organizations in the future. According to a recent survey conducted by Drake Beam Morin (DBM), a human capital consulting firm, 94 percent of North American human resource professionals say their organizations are inadequately preparing younger-generation employees to be senior leaders, at a time when sixty million baby boomers are expected to leave the workforce over the next fifteen years. This could spell severe manpower shortages and senior leadership gaps for unprepared companies. In addition, 40 percent of the two hundred professionals polled reported their companies were unsuccessful in encouraging collaboration between younger and older workers, further undermining younger employees' ability to successfully move into leadership positions.

Of course, I am making the assumption that emerging leaders *want* to move into leadership positions once offered. I am increasingly seeing situations in which my clients offer leadership roles to their high potentials, only to see them rejected. Maybe the high potentials don't want to relocate. Maybe they *like* the job they're doing now. Maybe they worry that they will be less successful in a more senior role. Maybe they fear having to behave like the leaders they've seen in similar more senior roles. Actually, I am seeing combinations of all of these situations. In one client system with an intimidating performance review process but no real mentoring, high potentials did not want to risk being in new positions over their heads without anyone to guide them, for fear of being fired.

My colleagues at Passages Consulting, Mindy Millward and Ulrich Nettesheim, are seeing the same trends. The CEOs and senior leaders we interact with in our consulting practice are wringing their hands in the search for qualified leaders to take on broader roles in their organizations. Though many have concluded the problem is just a matter of slim pickings, the issue is actually very different.

I set out several years back to understand the relationship between leaders in organizations and the impact they have on performance. I had already spent a good part of my professional life studying and writing about the relationships between leaders and those that advise them. Now I wanted to understand how the relationships between leaders and those they led served as a mechanism to drive transformation and performance in organizations. What I learned surprised me. I found no shortage of leaders. In fact, I found an abundance of them, in every corner of the organizations in which I searched. Enthusiastic, eager, outrageously smart, these women and men were hungry for the chance to put their fingerprints on the organizations in which they worked. And in the intervening time, they haven't vanished—they're in most organizations right now. These people are dying to lead, but with one catch: though they have a deep desire to step up and lead, they have *no* desire whatsoever to lead as they have been led. And most of today's incumbent leaders, having grown up with a very different paradigm of leadership, aren't able to recognize these emerging leaders and their immense potential. Why?

Because these young leaders don't look anything like their predecessors. Most leaders out scouring the planet for high potentials are naturally drawn to those who emulate the characteristics they think made them personally successful. They look for someone who both looks similar to them in background and embodies an executive hero, complete with cape and mask. When they don't see potential leaders who fit this bill, the easiest conclusion to draw is that there simply are no potential leaders in the pool. This conclusion is understandable, but misguided.

After talking with hundreds of incumbent and emerging leaders about this collision of voices, I believe there is a way forward besides giving up on one another. Let me try and bring some clarity to this rift. To put it in the extreme, incumbent leaders have concluded that the emerging generation of leaders are a bunch of overly emotional, touchy-feely, hypercreative radicals who lack the discipline to work in rigorous jobs, are strong willed and rebellious to a fault, have no respect for authority, and lack the work ethic necessary to contend in competitive marketplaces. By contrast, the emerging leaders have concluded that their predecessors have set a poor example of leadership, have relished the trappings of rank and exploited their position for personal gain, lack integrity, are workaholics, are manipulative and Machiavellian, and are unable to engage in anything more than superficial conversation, especially with anyone who differs from how they see the world.

Fortunately, I can say that neither point of view is accurate.

Yes, there are hints of partial truths in both perspectives. But both sides are needlessly throwing the proverbial baby out with perfectly good bathwater. I believe we can step back and have a different conversation. We can form relationships that respectfully leverage the differences each leader brings. And through those relationships, we can turn this seeming collision into a conversation that transforms organizations. We can eliminate the need for either leader to stoop to relying on suspicious speculation about what the other is thinking, with each searching for ways to out-maneuver the other. Let's see how.

DIVIDED: THE BAR IS EXPONENTIALLY HIGHER

The relentless rate of global change has created an unprecedented set of leadership requirements for today's executives. As my colleagues and I share our findings from client systems, however, I am convinced the new requirements are not being fully considered as companies seek to groom emerging leaders for the future.

To suggest leadership is about good relationships, on one hand, risks oversimplifying to an excessive degree. Focusing on good relationships seems to suggest a number of commonsense actions, such as the following:

- Being more courteous and considerate to those you lead
- Inviting your people into more decisions that affect them

- Expressing more interest in your people's aspirations and careers
- Providing some sage advice every now and then so the people you lead feel mentored
- Disclosing a bit more about yourself personally so you are a more credible leader
- Paying people more compliments and expressing greater appreciation for their contributions

For many, these actions would indeed qualify as highly effective leadership, especially when compared with either traditional command and control methods or the absentee leadership that has lingered in our corporations for decades. You might improve relationships with your dry cleaner or physician using these methods, but emerging leaders have simply grown unsatisfied with accepting the bare minimum these synthetic approaches imply. Leaders who stick to these actions are often well-meaning—and completely unaware that their behavior is being experienced as anything less than genuine.

I believe the requirements of leadership relationships, especially those between different generations, have more profound implications than just improving the series of interactions that are transacted in the course of a day. The crisis of leadership is not about the lack of an *ample supply* of leaders ready to lead. It is, rather, about the rapidly growing population of emerging leaders unwilling to tolerate the deteriorating standards of leadership to which they believe they have been subjected. Cultivating a crop of highly effective men and women ready to take on the mantle of leadership in today's context—and tomorrow's—will require engaging them in relationships of far deeper reach than they have experienced before in their workplaces. This requires building relationships of depth proportionate to the degrees of change and risk they will inherit in the organizations they will eventually lead.

A daunting challenge, to say the least.

Here's why. For starters, a recent survey on improving workplace relations found that fully 52 percent of employees in major U.S. corporations simply don't believe the information they receive from senior management. This statistic dovetails with a broader collapse of trust in authority figures throughout society. Public trust in the federal government, for example, has collapsed, generation to generation. In 1964, the American National Election Study reported that 75 percent of Americans said they trusted the federal government to do the right thing most of the time, but by 1996 that figure had fallen to 29 percent. During the fall of 2005, the nation's top oil executives were called to Capitol Hill to explain to a skeptical Congress that $4.00-a-gallon gas and multibillion-dollar surplus profits had nothing to do with price gouging in the wake of Hurricanes Katrina and Rita. Needless to say, America shared Congress's skepticism. Clearly, today's high potentials have grown up in an atmosphere of greater distrust, both inside their companies and throughout society at large.

Now add to this the staggering rates of change, introducing unprecedented uncertainty in the areas of globalization, emerging markets, technology, and dynamic consumer buying patterns. Forces such as insourcing and outsourcing, offshoring, and open sourcing have invited unprecedented numbers of new, unexpected entrants onto a global playing field. As technology jobs are regularly moved to India and China, Americans are having to compete for higher-wage jobs as never before. Middle people are being sliced out of every value chain to bring costs and prices down. Emerging leaders are having to form new types of relationships and networks in order to navigate their careers in a global neighborhood. And in this global neighborhood, trust is extended, or withheld, based on very different types of criteria than we've ever seen before.

Older executives have grown up in a world in which organizations made decisions about what to produce and supply. Considering the needs of others, customers or otherwise, was only moderately required. Younger executives are more in touch with a world in which substantial control has shifted into the hands of consumers, thus giving consumers the wherewithal to demand that they be marketed to in vastly different ways. New technologies have enabled consumers to manage and customize the relationship they have with producers of goods and services. Consumers are increasingly willing to abandon businesses who insist on doing business a certain way because "that's just the way we do it." The younger generation of executives *are* these new style consumers. They demand customization, insist on relevance to their own needs and desires, and reject outmoded distribution channels and procedures as consumers. If they are this way as consumers, why should they be any different as executives?

FROM GOOD TO GREAT . . . TO PRISON

Finally, we have to consider the cost of corporate failure, both financial and of reputation. New York State Attorney General Eliot Spitzer has made headline after headline systematically attacking corporate abuses. A visit to his office's website reads like a who's who of embarrassed corporations:

- In 2002, several top investment banks were accused of inflating stock prices and using affiliated brokerage firms to give biased investment advice. The banks paid $1.4 billion in compensation and fines. A sideshow to this suit unfolded in the media as the New York Stock Exchange itself came under scrutiny and the immense compensation package of NYSE CEO Richard Grasso turned into a major embarrassment. Grasso retired and was required to return a portion of his compensation.
- In 2003, mutual fund brokers came under fire for allowing select clients privileges not granted to ordinary customers, including allowing hedge fund investors to file trades at the previous day's price after the market close ("late trading") and "market timing," which allows privileged investors to buy and sell shares in funds more frequently than stipulated under the fund's rules. Marsh and McLennan's Putnam Investments was found to have engaged in both practices. The top leaders of Putnam resigned, and Marsh and McLennan joined several other companies paying in total over a billion dollars in fines.

The list goes on. What is interesting about these cases is that Spitzer is successfully taking corporations to task for practices that everybody agrees are indefensible on the ethical plane *but* that everybody also agrees have been happening for decades, in some instances hiding behind the notion that "it's not technically illegal."

It doesn't end there. The headlines are crowded with names of once respected leaders who have run afoul of the law. In some instances leaders have brazenly engaged in self-enriching schemes to the detriment of their companies, investors, employees, and pensioners. Adelphia's John Rigas, for example, turned a $300 license into an $18 billion cable empire, and were it not for the end of his story, he'd look like the poster child for entrepreneurial leadership. Unfortunately, Rigas wound up sentenced to fifteen years in prison after bilking the company of over $100 million and leaving it bankrupt.

In other instances, leaders have encouraged illegal practices to curry favor with important constituencies. An article on a recent *Wall Street Journal* front page read: "Volkswagen, Europe's biggest automaker and one of Germany's corporate icons, illegally used company funds to pay for top labor leaders to go on junkets involving posh hotels, call girls, and the use of a company plane. Mr. Gebauer, former mid level manager in the company's personnel department, claims he was given blanket instruction by his boss to use the trips to curry worker representatives' support for Volkswagen management."

Faith-based leaders, typically held up as moral exemplars in their community, are not exempt. High-profile stories of Jim Bakker's adultery with Jessica Hahn or the numerous allegations against Catholic priests make national headlines, and according to one study by *Leadership Journal,* the statistic that four pastors in ten may have had a major moral failure explains countless local stories of impropriety.

See the problem? Accumulated stories of great leaders gone bad don't inspire a lot of confidence in emerging leaders waiting in the wings. The pool of people from which the next generation of leaders must come will be inheriting unparalleled degrees of risk from a population of leaders they are trusting less and less. Instead of taking the reins with passion and confidence, eager to push their organizations to new heights, they will be hesitant, cautiously watching their backs, and trying to avoid any misstep that could derail their organization, or worse, their career. Not exactly a recipe for success. Many are simply saying "no thanks" to the opportunity—and it is easy to see why.

The seemingly endless sequence of horrifying stories about leaders and organizations who have failed thanks to either poor judgment or an alarming lack of integrity has left today's and tomorrow's leaders bereft of hope. Whether it's a CEO who embezzles funds or a pastor who commits adultery, it seems as if we meet a new failed leader in the press every week—someone who has covered up, tampered with, overlooked, or hidden some issue or set of issues, in the deluded hope things would all work out. Now, the media is on a witch hunt to dig up the next "caught with pants down" leader who presides over a scandal at some enterprise and whose immense compensation flies in the face of the damage done.

The unfortunate issue here is that many leaders face some risk of guilt by association, rightly or wrongly, especially from emerging leaders. My twenty years of experience working alongside wonderful and brilliant men and women at the top level of organizations tells me there are many more good apples than bad. They would sincerely like to inspire far greater leadership performance by telling their stories of both transformational triumphs as well as failures. I think there is minimal value to be gained by continuing to provoke fear and pessimism with the stories of leaders whose reprehensible actions became nothing more than tabloid failures, leaving behind a wake of heartbroken people, disappointed shareholders, and vengeful analysts.

And here's an example. In the list above, the story of Marsh and McLennan hits close to home for me. They were the parent company of the firm I worked at for nearly eight years. It was painfully shameful for me to hear of the stories brought to light about a company at which I was employed. But I was also employed there on September 11, 2001, when MMC lost nearly three hundred employees when a plane crashed into the World Trade Center. In the months that followed, I saw the MMC community rally in phenomenal ways around families and colleagues who were frightened and grieving. We manned hot lines, helped families locate loved ones, shared offices with those who no longer had a place to work, cried with grieving spouses and parents, gave tens of millions of dollars, and together, mourned a gruesome tragedy. How is it that an organization accused of corrupt business practices could at the same time rise to extraordinary and heroic heights to care for its community?

Is that not the paradox of all leaders and organizations? That we are all capable of acting both in ways that fill others with passionate hope—and in ways that appall others into harsh cynicism?

My hope in writing this book is to inspire and challenge all of us—emerging and incumbent leaders alike—to participate in a new conversation about what is possible, in both relationship and performance. My dream is to see us live nobly within these paradoxical tensions of organizational life.

Only in relationship can we find the courage and grace to live as leaders who neither ignore or abet cruelty or corruption, nor fail to celebrate and honor the beauty and goodness we create or experience. To live seeing life through rose-colored glasses, only accentuating the positive in the world of organizational leadership, is cowardly. To live only in contempt, throwing daggers at the evils of corrupted power and greed, is also cowardly.

To live with both, in the absolute mystery of their contradictions, takes compassion and guts.

I found many wonderful stories among those of great difference persevering in relationships and finding their way to surprising common ground. It was there they found innovative ideas and extraordinary results they otherwise would have forfeited had they abandoned their pursuit of one another. The first step is simply staying in the game. Once on the playing field, however, leaders must start with the assumption that "all that I see isn't all there is to see." This book aspires to help you see and to lead into relationships of extraordinary value.

CONNECTING THE RELATIONSHIP DOTS

I join my colleagues in having a somewhat unique vantage point for understanding leader relationships. As consultants, we search the halls of the organizations in which we do our work, looking for insights and ideas in the service of some great change. A substantial part of this job is "dot connecting." Because our work affords us the privilege of a free passport across organizational borders that would be closed to insiders, we have the chance to perceive patterns (both productive and unproductive) that would not likely be visible to a member of the organization. Unlike insiders who live in just one silo and rarely get to, or choose to, experience other units of the organization, we can detect issues that span the enterprise, potentially hindering organizational performance. We also have the opportunity to see latent capacity that, if coherently leveraged, could advance otherwise floundering strategies. These patterns often tell a powerful story that, when stitched together, arms leaders with insight to act in creative ways that bring greater capability and coherence to often fragmented and disabled organizations.

The patterns we see in the relationships among leaders often tell the most revealing stories. Usually the symptoms show up first. Logistics can't get orders shipped to customers on time, and the supply chain organization can't get manufacturing to work with sales to get better forecasts. The finance organization is trying to get operations to cut costs, and operations is trying to get finance to free up more resources, but nobody is talking with anyone else; everyone is just lobbing "scud messages" over the wall at each other. The head of marketing is launching promotions without warning the sales regions about what's coming. The division head has some new idea and has whipped the entire senior team into a frenzy of activity—resentfully seen as the *idea du jour.* The senior pastor of the church is being pressured by the board to add services and grow, but his staff is complaining about being overworked and underresourced. The executive director of the urban youth center has asked her staff to work more hours on weekends during the summer months but cannot offer commensurate pay for the sacrifice because of budget shortfalls. The superintendent of schools has asked all teachers to serve on school improvement committees, and though most don't believe any good will come of them, they go through the motions anyway.

At the heart of these symptoms I find relationships that at best are ill formed and more often are in various stages of disarray. Some have been family feuds for years that have been ignored as inconsequential to performance. Conversely, when I see leaders working exceptionally well, producing extraordinary results, we can always detect a set of relationships that are vibrant and engaging. The quality of genuine conversation among leaders in such relationships is different. It's animated. It's focused. It's bold. It's inclusive. Clearly, underneath whatever issues are being wrestled with, whatever opportunities are being seized, important relationships are being honored and strengthened.

In the research for this book, we found at least six patterns that distinguished distressed relationships from powerful relationships. I would certainly never suggest these are *the* patterns of high-performing relationships. Too many books on this topic have reduced leadership to simplistic recipes—ten steps, eight secrets, fifteen laws, twelve habits, fifty principles, nine competencies, and on and on. Wonderful lists of attributes meant to describe what it is good leaders *do to others* fall short of the mark for one reason: they imply that the participation of those around the leader is immaterial. Leadership is not something one does *to* someone else. Rather, it is something one does *with* someone else. History, literature, and academia have done us a disservice by focusing on leaders as heroic, stand-alone individuals. True leadership is not a solo act. And it is our history's obsessive pursuit of *individualism* that, paradoxically, I believe has eclipsed the true *uniqueness of individuals.* We have homogenized the generic population of followers as though they were a commodity, while focusing on the individual leader guiding that population. It's time to stop—no, really stop—the notion of leadership as a *person* and engage in the more accurate notion of leadership as a *relationship.* More often than not, it is a complex portfolio of relationships, each one distinctive and complex in its own right. The truly effective leader adapts to these individuals, building relationships with them that give rise to creativity, sustainable solutions to difficult problems, and enhanced levels of trust and performance. It is this process of continuously investing in ever-deepening *relationships* that comprises leadership, not the techniques one does or doesn't employ.

The six patterns we discovered most frequently are consistent with my experience and the experience of my colleagues. There could well be dozens more, and you should add your own to the list. I simply chose to draw attention to these because of the recurring frequency with which they appeared. You may decide that it was an arbitrary place to stop forming the list, and you could well be right. My hope is to *start* a conversation that will keep going. There is much to say on this issue, and I hope others will enter the conversation with conviction so that we can prepare the next generation of leaders with the confidence and care they deserve.

Each of the chapters in the book is formed around one of these patterns. I hope that the exploration of each will inspire change among organizational leaders of all kinds. Table I.1 summarizes the patterns or the *needs* of leaders and the opportunity that each represents.

TABLE I.1. THE SIX PATTERNS: WHAT LEADERS NEED.

The Leadership Need	From—To	Opportunity
A Level Playing Field	The death of rank—the dare of exposure	Neutralize hierarchy to *accelerate trust and results*
A Great Cup of Coffee	The death of veneer—the dare of depth	Have deeper conversations, not better transactions, to *surface innovative and dangerous thinking*
A Voice at the Table	The death of deception—the dare of invitation	Extend genuine invitations, dispense with faux involvement, to *maximize passion and commitment*
An Imaginative Dream	The death of monotony—the dare of dreaming	Dream first, set targets later, to *push leaders to the limits of their capability*
A Diamond in Formation	The death of arrogance—the dare of generosity	Participate and contribute generously, stop doling out advice, to *engage leaders in an exploration of deep development*
A Grateful Champion	The death of patronizing—the dare of gratitude	Be more grateful, less complimentary, to *sustain courage and endurance*

UNDIVIDED: WHO GOES FIRST?

So, are we just at an impasse that's dividing incumbent and emerging leaders? If we believe the next generation of leaders is at stake and the future of our most vibrant organizations is threatened, then of course the answer has to be a resounding "no." Global corporations, universities, faith-based communities, not-for-profit agencies, NGOs, and public schools will need leaders in the coming years—leaders who must come from the emerging generation. The only question is, "Who goes first?"

Is it the incumbent leaders who must bend their ways and adapt to the unique needs and characteristics of the emerging leaders they are leading? Or is it the emerging leaders who must let go of their high expectations and ideals, learn what they can from the leaders leading them, and—for those who have the stamina to persevere—wait their turn for a chance at the helm? Well, I suppose the simple answer has to be somewhere in the middle—but not the exact middle. If we are to move this challenge along and start connecting these leaders with one another in productive and meaningful ways, the hand of invitation must first be extended by incumbent leaders to the up-and-coming leaders of tomorrow. And if they do this with genuineness and care, with an acknowledgment that they don't have all the answers and are willing to learn in the service of these emerging leaders' futures, then emerging leaders will respond with an enthusiastic hand back. They will be willing to let go of their cynical suspicions and some of the impulsivity that accompanies their impatience, to gain the great benefits of learning alongside those who have come before them. Today's leaders must allow many of the once-useful approaches of management to die and dare to allow a more relevant look at organizational leadership to evolve in the wake of their obsolescence. In so doing, they will secure the greatest possible legacy they can bestow: tomorrow's leaders prepared to perform even greater feats than today's.

Risky? Most likely. Worth a shot? Unquestionably. I've seen extraordinary things happen in organizations when leaders come alongside other leaders in the pursuit of audacious results that come about only through equally audacious relationships. And I have found it to be especially true between seasoned leaders and tomorrow's leaders. My hope is that this book will enable leaders to navigate the messy, unpredictable whitewater of vibrant relationships and to help build the confidence and capability needed to create them. It will require both participants in the relationship to at times be the *leading voice* and at other times to *lead the voices of others* into leadership. Sometimes you will be the wind, and other times you will be the sail. If you are willing to risk crossing your own divide toward adaptability, vulnerability, and trust, then I promise you an adventurous journey through the book.

Before we begin, let's meet some of the folks you will be getting better acquainted with as you read.

LET'S MEET THE PLAYERS

It's important for you to understand the voices that constitute the foundation of this book. I instructed the research team who joined me for this phase of the work to cast the net wide deliberately, to hear as many stories from leaders as possible. The goal of the research was not to quantify the challenge of a widening gap, but rather to understand that gap and how to close it. So I hope that telling the stories, both heartwarming and heartbreaking, of leaders from all sorts of organizations will help inform a point of view about the relationships between them.

Here is how the information was collected over the course of two years:

- In-depth interviews with more than sixty senior executives who presided over major corporations, non-profits, universities, and faith-based organizations, some of whose stories are recounted just as they were told
- An essay survey conducted with more than eleven hundred leaders, both incumbent and emerging, asking them to describe their experiences as leaders working together
- An essay survey conducted with M.B.A. students from the University of Washington Business School
- An essay survey conducted with the Northwestern University Alumni Association
- Extensive secondary research spanning business, clinical, sociological, faith-based, and journal literature

The stories and quotes you will hear throughout the book are true. In some cases, where anonymity was important, the names have been modified but the story left intact. I felt it was important for you to hear exactly what I heard. I am grateful to all those leaders who took the time to write and tell us of their experiences, their hopes, their frustrations, and to share their ideas. Regardless of the story, one thing I heard among these brave leaders was certain: they are all hungry for more. Ironically, they hunger for experiences they will find only in each other. And my sense is they are willing to do what it takes to find those experiences in one another, even if it's hard. Listen to what we heard from across the country and from within your organizations:

- "Leaders need to know when to let go of relationship for the task at hand and—more important—when to recognize when the relationship is more important than the task. True leadership wisdom is a balancing of the 'what' with the 'who.'"
- "I've had leaders who've had no concept of relationship. So when hard conversations needed to take place, or tough issues needed to be discussed, or even when someone was hurting, there was no relational 'capital' built up. So it was, at best, awkward. And at worst—well, it was ugly."
- "Leaders are the loneliest people there are. We don't even have anyone to admit that to. But we are desperate for relationships. It's easy to become isolated when you are in a big job. It's just hard to anticipate the terrible consequences of that isolation."
- "Without relationship—pure, authentic relationship—nothing happens."

As a way of sharing a summary of these two populations—incumbent and emerging leaders—Table I.2 presents a *very general* comparison of both groups. Summaries like this can be dangerous because they can quickly become stereotypes. The vastness of these two groups and the variation within each of them is significant, and the range of their views and ideas was amazing. So this should not serve as more than a high-level sense of some general patterns we detected from their stories. But it will give you a feel for what has been implicit in workplaces for many years—and is now gathering steam as a potential collision of great proportions, if we don't figure out how to build a bridge between them of mutual respect, curiosity, acceptance, and generative performance.

By way of *very loosely* identifying who these leaders are, let me simply (perhaps simplistically) say that *emerging leaders* are "up and comers." Most are in their twenties and thirties, some in their early forties. They are "on the rise" and in formation. *Incumbent leaders* are the seasoned veterans with many years of experience; most are in their mid- to late forties or fifties, or older. Age classifications are dangerously

TABLE I.2. COMPARISON OF INCUMBENT AND EMERGING LEADERS.

	Incumbent Leaders	Emerging Leaders
Rank	Have overly relied on hierarchy to make decisions, but have tried to resist command and control. Have made strides to distribute power in the organization and use hierarchy only as a means of clarifying roles. Many still struggle with their use of authority.	Avoid the use of rank as a means of decision making and influence. Seek to build consensus among many and to leverage diverse points of view. For many, having power is terrifying, and some can shy away from very tough decisions, for fear of being seen as dictatorial. Very aware of and sensitive to judgment from leaders. Discomfort with authority when they must exercise it outside the approval of others.
Meaningful Conversation	Less comfortable with emotionally laden language and anything that feels "personal." Meaning is defined by results and clarity, not by connection. The dawn of the concept of eQ has enabled some to progress and become more facile with a warmer way of relating.	Very comfortable expressing emotion and dealing with emotions of others. Become suspicious of those who seem emotionally guarded and won't self-disclose. Sometimes struggle with appropriate boundaries.
Inclusion/ Engagement	Have learned through dozens of team-building sessions the importance of including others in decisions that affect them. Many have learned to let the reins loosen, but struggle with not having "the answer" in their hip pocket. Risk being perceived as manipulative when stuck between wanting to do things their way but still wanting others to buy in.	Want everyone to enjoy the party equally. Have limitless patience for lengthy decisions that allow for all voices to be heard. Happy to allow others a say in many areas, even those that don't pertain to them. Invite others just for the sake of inclusion. Risk paralysis and momentum loss owing to excessive involvement by many.

	Incumbent Leaders	Emerging Leaders
Dreaming	Believe that performance is about setting goals, monitoring progress, and measuring results—and if you need training, get training. Think setting targets and following process is important as long as it doesn't invite needless bureaucracy. Think it's fine to allow others to have a vision as long as they keep commitments.	Could dream for days, and see most processes as unnecessarily bureaucratic and inhibiting creativity. Very idealistic, they have a passion for a cause and want to achieve things of greatness. Have a tendency to be impulsive with decisions and goals, not valuing the importance of data to inform choices. May struggle with holding others accountable for unmet commitments.
Generosity	Place a premium on developing those they most believe will in turn contribute to the organization. Can more easily distinguish performance levels among team members. Are happy to answer questions and serve as the "answer ATM" and enjoy helping others solve problems. Sometimes gratified by having others take their solutions. Can be a bit blunt and awkward when giving developmental feedback. Not comfortable disclosing personal shortcomings or failures.	Want to treat others with more equality and give liberally and evenly of their time and experience to others. Are hungry to learn from the experiences and insights of incumbent leaders but without the expectation that they must "do it like I do." Want to hear about their failures as well as their successes. Have strong fears of failure because their dreams are so large. Want someone to "guide them" but can be willful when it comes to doing it "their way." Want their voice to count in the lives of incumbent leaders as well.
Gratitude	Want to enthusiastically reward a job well done. Are glad to write memos or give public recognition for results to achievers. Appreciation is more commonly offered in exchange for outcomes, not simply for capability. Often excessive performance orientation can lead to being harsh or withholding appreciation when results are lackluster. Sincere compliments are offered as expressions of gratitude.	Want a champion who will cheer them on, and care deeply for their talent and their results. They want to be appreciated for who they are as much as for what they do. And they don't want the appreciation to fade when the results aren't there. They need a lot of encouragement to stay in the game, and their feelings of uncertainty can be consuming if they feel they've lost ground in their leader's eyes.

rudimentary because they can be overly narrowing, but generally speaking these are the ranges into which these populations fell.

WELCOME TO BROOKREME TECHNOLOGIES

One of the most powerful ways we all learn is through story. And sometimes the best way to really look in the mirror at our own story is to first look into the story of another. You might be wondering how the story of Jack and Randy that began this chapter plays out. You'll have to resolve that for yourself—and you will when you have that conversation with a fellow leader in your organization. I want to give you a deeper and more complete look at the relationships I'm talking about by introducing you to the somewhat fictionalized senior executives at Brookreme Technologies, a global technology corporation. You'll get to know them quite well as you read the book. Each of the six patterns will be viewed and viewed again, through the world of Brookreme. This is an archetypal corporation. It comprises all common patterns and behaviors we have seen in real corporations. You will come to enjoy and, in some cases, be quite frustrated with these leaders. They, like you, are doing the best work they can. They have a daunting strategic challenge in front of them. You get a front-row seat to the relationships among them and how those relationships do or don't serve their aspirations. I hope you will come to enjoy and appreciate these leaders as you get to know them—and will wrestle with their challenges as if they were your own.

ESTUARY

An estuary is a wide body of water formed where a large river converges with the sea. It contains both freshwater and saltwater. It is a confluence of forces that normally would never cohabit without destructive elements. But in this unique habitat, two completely different water types and sources come together and form one of the most sensitive and ecologically important environments on Earth, one that provides sanctuary to diverse forms of wildlife, some of which could survive in no other place. It is interesting to note, by contrast, that one definition of a *divide* is a body of water that starts in one place and flows in two opposite directions. Today, many relationships between incumbent and emerging leaders are much like a divide, moving in opposite directions from one another.

The voices of incumbent and emerging leaders need to become an estuary of sorts. Today they are struggling to converge productively in organizations in a way that can help them move from their divide to create something powerful and unique they could not create on their own. The pages ahead will help you navigate the headwaters of your own estuary and create blended leadership voices that, undivided, will serve as a powerful, performance-driving force in your organization.

For those of you with the courage to do so, I highly recommend you choose a counterpart with whom to read this book. If you are an incumbent leader, reach out to an emerging leader with whom you work and with whom you might enjoy a stronger relationship. Offer to read the book and discuss it together. If you are an emerging leader, reach out to an incumbent leader and do the same thing. I promise you that the ensuing experience will be more transformational than anything on the pages ahead.

And one final note on design. You'll see throughout the book quotes and callouts with fascinating statistics and facts, as well as artifacts of culture—songs, poems, movies, and the like. My guess would be that if you are an incumbent leader you will naturally be drawn to the places where you see the decimal points and percentage symbols. And if you are an emerging leader you will be drawn to the poets, songwriters, movies, and literature. This is by design—with one twist. My challenge to you is to explore the ones you are *least* drawn to. (Don't worry, nobody has to know that as a CEO you read a quote from an obscure philosopher or pop icons like Bono or David Brent from the BBC series *The Office*. If you are a twenty-something youth pastor or a thirty-something rising executive, your friends don't have to know you enjoyed reading about the profitability and EPS performance of a global corporation.) If you are truly going to learn about one another and begin to appreciate the cultures that have shaped each other's thinking and behavior, then you need to begin to welcome the information that has influenced and formed each of you. Like the dynamic notations written above the lines of a music score, guiding musicians on how to interpret the music's *sound,* not just the *notes,* so too can these symbols help you interpret the *sound* of a culture that has been somewhat unfamiliar to you, not just the *pieces* of it. So try it. You may unearth some pleasant surprises your eyes might otherwise have been inclined to pass over.

Not to overstate the obvious, but I'm assuming that having picked this up, you have a more than moderate appetite for building leadership relationships that inspire great results with others. Presumably, then, you are also open to being inspired. If you can remain open to soaking up the lessons of these leaders and their relationships with other leaders, chances are good you'll allow something from their stories to awaken within *you* something that inspires greater performance in others. And if that happens, I'll consider our time together well worth it—and I hope you will too.

Let's get started.

CHAPTER ONE

A LEVEL PLAYING FIELD

The Death of Rank, The Dare of Exposure

When fortune surprises us by giving us an important position, without having led us to it by degrees, or without our being elevated to it by our hopes, it is almost impossible for us to maintain ourselves suitably in it, and appear worthy of possessing it.

La Rochefoucauld, *Maxims*

Opportunity: Neutralize hierarchy to accelerate trust and results.

Have you ever found yourself in this quandary?

The team flocked into the conference room with a noticeable level of nervous energy. Nancy, Brookreme Corporation's seasoned CEO of seven years, had summoned her management committee to an unexpected meeting, telling them only that a major opportunity was on the horizon. Of course, Nancy's vague statement created quite a hallway buzz as the team members ravenously hunted for any morsels of information on what this major opportunity might be. The head of strategy told the CFO he knew nothing about any imminent deals. The sales executive cornered the head of HR to see if she knew of some strategic hire coming on board. The head of R&D marched into the COO's office and demanded to know if he'd leaked some of the "highly confidential" major initiatives on the drawing board. It was clear Nancy had something very important to tell the team, and whatever it was, nobody had a clue—or at least nobody was letting on if they did.

Nancy was on her cell phone at the back of the room as the team filed in. Some sat, others stood against the wall. Anxious glances were exchanged while the team waited for Nancy to finish her call. Nobody could make out what she was saying because she was clearly speaking softly, which was unusual for Nancy. When she finished, she snapped her cell phone shut, turned, leaned forward, and said, "OK, team, here's the situation. I've been thinking about this for a long time, and the more I've studied the opportunity, the more I'm convinced we need to have a presence in China. I know we've debated this on and off. But with the increasing power of the Chinese economy, I think we could find ourselves in an unwinnable price war if we don't move now. Just look at how fast technology is migrating to Shanghai. Alchatech just announced they are opening manufacturing facilities there next year and will follow with distribution from Hong Kong and Singapore within the next two years. This is huge. They've already taken one of our major customers this year. If we don't build the capacity to supply global customers like them, and take cost out of the process, then we're gonna continue to take hits.

"So here's what I want," Nancy continued. "Don, I'd like you to assemble a SWAT team and start an intense feasibility study to determine what it would take for us to go after new or deeper relationships in the Pacific Rim. I want to know if we should open a sales office in Hong Kong, or if we'd be better off in Seoul or even Shanghai. I know this is going to piss off our people in Sydney because they've been going after this for a couple of years and have resisted us moving physically into Southeast Asia. But let me deal with that. Jim, I'll want your help since they report to you."

Addressing the whole team, Nancy said, "I know this feels sudden, and maybe even impulsive to you. But you have to trust my gut on this one, and I need your support to make it happen. I don't want to be asked at the next board meeting what our thoughts are on responding to Alchatech's move without having a robust response. I'm already getting emails from some of them asking why we didn't see this coming. Any questions?"

Don had plenty of questions, but he didn't open his mouth. Instead he seethed internally, barely containing his outrage. Don had been head of strategy for Brookreme for just under three years. His Harvard M.B.A. afforded him an early rise to the C-suite, and at just thirty-seven he had been enjoying the chance to influence strategic direction. But over the course of the past several months he and Nancy had had some heated debates regarding Asia. Don had strong misgivings. He worried that Nancy had underestimated both the market volatility of the region and the enormous cultural implications of doing business there. Don felt that Brookreme risked its credibility with U.S. and European markets—not to mention competitors like the Korean or Japanese who already had strong footholds in the region. An overnight decision like this seemed an unwarranted risk to Don. His face clearly betrayed his internal angst.

The team hustled out twice as fast as they had arrived. Nancy signaled Jim, her calm and always collected COO, to stay behind. The door was barely closed before Nancy yelled, "Why the hell does he do that?"

Jim knew what she meant, and he knew *who* she meant, too.

"I know he doesn't want to do this, but for crying out loud, don't stand in the middle of the room looking at the floor, sulking, looking away and drawing attention to your disagreement when you're the damn head of strategy!" Nancy shouted. "Open up your damn mouth and say something if you have a problem, but don't pocket veto in front of everyone."

Nancy slumped back in her chair and continued, "This is what I get for putting a kid in diapers in such a big job. And I know exactly where he is right now. Fifty bucks says he's down in Anita's office this very moment whining about me and what I've asked him to do. I'm sick of this crap, Jim. I'm just sick of it. Don is a talented kid, no question. But when the hell is he going to grow up and stop bucking me at every turn? I swear, everything takes five times longer to get done when you have to deal with this nonsense."

Jim perched on the edge of the table in a fatherly pose, ready to talk Nancy down off the "what to do about Don" ledge. "Don't let this fester, Nancy," he said. "You need to go down there right now and talk with him. Don't *scream* at him, though. Just *talk* to him. He knows you're the boss, you've made that clear. But *listen* to him. Some of his concerns may have merit. If you don't want him to behave like a kid, maybe you shouldn't keep treating him like one."

Regardless of whether Nancy was handling Don the right way, her suspicion of what he was doing was perfectly on target. While she was venting to Jim, Don was indeed down in Anita's office doing the same thing.

"How the hell could she do something like this?" Don asked heatedly. "At least she could show me the respect of clueing me in *before* she tells the whole team. She knows how I feel, so instead of being direct with me, she just pulls rank and end-runs me. If she's not going to let me be her damn head of strategy, fine. But let's stop pretending. I've done nothing but stand up and salute any time she asks for something. This time I'm not going to just roll over. This time she's done her top-down thing once too often. I'm not just some snot-nosed green kid with a newly-minted M.B.A. right off the school bus. I know what I'm talking about. CEO or not, she ought to at least give me some credit. And I know she's in there right now complaining to Jim about me.

Jim's told me that she vents to him about me whenever I try to exert any influence at all. What does she expect me to do—just blindly carry out her orders when she barks them?"

Venting helped Don calm down a little, but he had hardly taken two steps out of Anita's door when he walked right into Nancy. Without missing a beat, she said to him, "Oh, Don, glad I found you. Let's step into your office for a minute. I want to follow up on the China conversation."

For the Moment

What's your hunch about how this conversation will play out?

Do you find yourself identifying more with Nancy or Don? Jim or Anita? Why?

How would the team meeting have been different if you were in the room?

This story gets at an issue that's complicated, as most issues of relationship are. On one hand, Nancy *is* the CEO, and she has the clear responsibility to set direction and pursue opportunities she feels are critical to Brookreme's success. On the other hand, she's appointed someone she feels brings important perspective to the strategic direction of the company, and she's now chosen to reject his views without letting him know her decision in advance. This is her prerogative—she doesn't *have* to take Don's advice. But Nancy has done so in a public forum, leaving Don feeling outranked and disenfranchised right in front of his peers. At the same time, Nancy feels unsupported and undermined. Will the two of them find a way, as colleagues, to set aside the confinement of their respective roles long enough to search for common ground? We'll check in with them again at the end of the chapter after considering what a level playing field might actually look like.

> *The GDP (Gross Domestic Product) of the poorest 48 nations (i.e. a quarter of the world's countries) is less than the wealth of the world's three richest* people *combined.*
> IGNACIO RAMONET
> *The Politics of Hunger*

A RANK HISTORY OF PRIVILEGE

For centuries, the process of organizing human endeavor has required the use of hierarchy to delineate the varying roles leaders play, especially in a complex system of multiple interacting parts. Since the days of feudal caste systems and early military formations, rank has been an important device for clarifying who's deciding what and who follows whom. People in medieval and early modern times literally equated social roles with functions of the body, with the ruling class cast as the society's mind and the laboring class cast as arms and legs. Monarchs became so closely identified with their roles as chief executives of their nations that they were said to have two bodies: the physical body every person has and a second, mystical body that was the realization of the king's function. Curiously, modern corporations are, in law, exactly this sort of a nonphysical "body" that represents the corporate function and is treated as a separate person, distinct from investors, officers, or workers. The very word *corporation* comes from *corpus,* the Latin word for "body." Before the revolutions of the modern period, most people gave no more thought to questioning authority than they would to asking if their own hands and feet should obey their heads.

The corporate body was always conceived of as a group of people gathered together in a command hierarchy, acting in concert as a separate corporate identity. The structure mirrored the other command hierarchies of the time, which placed a premium on executive leadership. Modern corporations came of age in the seventeenth century at a time when a lot of modern arrangements, be they military, political, or economic, were taking shape. In fact, the navy hierarchy was taking its modern shape in Great Britain just at the time that modern concepts of equity and debt financing and corporate organization were finding expression. It is no coincidence that the individuals vested with responsibility for running the corporation are called *officers* as opposed to something like *agents* or *deputies* or *representatives.* Corporate officers have traditionally had a much stronger leadership role than merely acting as the custodians of shareholders' interests. Somehow, top corporate officers had to pull in large amounts of capital, build factories, get labor working, and connect to markets. To the organizers of early corporations, running an enterprise and leading a military campaign presented similar logistical challenges, and the command and control techniques used in one field were valid in the other.

You don't have to go back to the seventeenth century to see this cross-fertilization in action. The Whiz Kids who ran the Ford Motor Company in the 1950s (including the first Ford CEO who was not himself a member of the Ford family, Robert McNamara) were all young men in the service during the Second World War, whose ideas of scientific management, hierarchical command structure, delegation of authority, audit, and control came straight from the U.S. Army. The science of managing this hierarchy and ruthlessly pruning it for maximum efficiency continues today at Crotonville. The popularity of Jack Welch's books underscores how firmly these ideas still are rooted in American business.

Certainly, scientifically managed hierarchies have achieved considerable successes and created great value in business. But there has been a flaw built into them from the very beginning: hierarchy as a device for delineating roles risks becoming entwined with defining power, status, and importance. Indeed, until fairly recently the people at the apex of political, military, and business hierarchies actively courted pomp and outward symbols of their authority. As the compensation levels of a corporation's most senior leaders have skyrocketed in recent years, the emblems of power and privilege have become as important for top executives as they once were for monarchs—lushly appointed offices, the 1950s dawn of the executive washroom, company-provided luxury cars, an entourage of staff assistants, corporate jets, and boondoggles to tropical paradises for five hours of meetings and three days of golf and spa treatments. You could be forgiven for mistaking today's corporate leaders for the nobles of pre-revolutionary France—and the scary thing is that the income disparity between rich and poor in twenty-first-century America is actually larger than that between nobles and peasants in eighteenth-century France. The pride and callousness of these French aristocrats preceded a fall that changed the course of organizational history. Might we be next?

I recently heard a story about a leader in an organization complaining about how he couldn't get a deal on a new, rare European watch and was forced to pay the full price of $32,000 for the one he wanted. In the same conversation, he spoke about the frustrations of how much it cost to maintain his yacht and his antique car collection. Things were so rough that he was actually considering selling one of his vacation properties. This leader's complaints would be considered insensitive by even the most privileged among us. However, his comments were made even more remarkable by the fact that he aired them in the midst of a staff meeting among women and men who made a tiny fraction of his salary.

His staff was forced to nod in feigned sympathy at his harrowing conundrum. Later in the meeting, when one of them talked about taking her family to the Jersey shore for vacation, he said, "C'mon, are you kidding me? That's not a vacation! You should treat your family better than that. Have you done Maui yet? If not, it's fantastic for families there. And you can get a great deal on a three-thousand square foot, two-bedroom house, fully staffed, right on the beach for probably $20,000 for a week, off season." That suggestion represented about 25 percent of the woman's annual salary. At that moment, his secretary came in and said, "Your driver is waiting for you, and your wife called and said she'd meet you at the airport. She has to pick up the nanny first, and she wanted to know if you remembered to pack your diving license." As this executive's team members all left the meeting, one sarcastically muttered to the others, "I hope I live long enough to have those kinds of problems." The woman said, "Remind me never to talk about my vacation plans with him again. I should have known better."

Anyone could read that story and shudder at such incredible inconsiderateness. But being out of touch with others is a natural byproduct of climbing a hierarchy—and it will create challenging barriers to any relationship if you're not careful. The subtle signals of self-importance and self-aggrandizement are far more revealing than any leader would ever want to believe. Sadly, this story isn't as rare as you might hope.

The trappings of rank have nothing to do with the number of layers on the organization chart. The reengineering craze of the 1980s and 1990s stripped dozens of layers from organizations in the hunt for speed and efficiency. Even though many organizations found greater economies of scale in technologically driven processes and dropped percentage points to their bottom lines, "flattening" their structure did little to reduce the impact of rank-based thinking on the organization's performance. This does seem counterintuitive at first. Reengineering's tireless champion, Michael Hammer, is a terrifically persuasive speaker, and his argument that far too much time is wasted passing tasks from one group to another makes sense. Hammer points out that it is far more efficient to appoint a team responsible for all the tasks in a given process, either inside the company or outside, including suppliers, distributors, and other business partners. But there is a persistent problem with this. Even at the height of the reengineering craze in the 1990s, various commentators claimed that as many as 85 percent of all reengineering efforts were outright failures. Even CSC Index, the original Hammer promulgator of consulting services, estimated that two-thirds of reengineering efforts yielded "mediocre, marginal, or failed results." Hammer himself has acknowledged the difficulties inherent in re-engineering, and he attributes them to poor execution of the necessary changes. I take issue with this—though clearly some change efforts are botched in execution, the success rate should still be higher than it is if getting rid of layers and handoffs actually works.

I think the real answer is that the de-layering pursuit is only half right. The notion that speed is a byproduct of reducing people's unnecessary participation in business processes—especially decision making—is true. Establishing processes and technology to move information only to those places it is most needed is a great way of getting the right people to act more quickly to resolve issues or seize opportunities. Indeed, greater organizational clarity can both reduce decision paralysis and mitigate the information traffic jams caused by political battles or diffuse accountability.

The flaw in the theory is the notion that broadening spans of control and having fewer layers between the top and bottom of an organization is the way to achieve greater clock speed. True, fewer layers might *facilitate* that speed. But picture in your mind this kind of leader:

- Inclined to micromanage
- Flaunts privileges and drops names
- Insists on participating in decisions they really shouldn't
- Directs the work of others even though those employees are presumably entrusted with key decisions
- Exercises every bit of the authority that comes with the role, no matter how trivial

It doesn't really matter how many or how few layers are underneath this kind of leader—things are going to slow down.

Some have argued for simply doing away with hierarchy all together. Perhaps the foremost proponent of this view is Jeffrey Nielsen, who calls for an end to rank-based hierarchies in his book *The Myth of Leadership: Creating Leaderless Organizations.* According to Nielsen, hierarchies should be replaced by a peer-based leadership model. Nielsen feels there is a qualitative difference between rank-based thinking and peer-based thinking, with the former based on a monopoly of information and control at the top of a hierarchy and the latter based on the belief that everyone in the organization should have equal standing to share in information, participate in the decision-making process, and choose to follow through persuasive means. He posits that a peer-based organization would be free of the miscommunication, corruption, and abuses of power inherent in top-down leadership systems. This organization would also be essentially leaderless.

But is hierarchy really the problem? Would anarchy be any better? Can every decision be made by group consensus, without someone ultimately accountable for a strategic decision or direction? Frankly, I don't believe hierarchy in and of itself is the issue. I think there is something deeper going on—and the lingering effects of command-and-control leadership and the intolerance of emerging leaders are starting to spotlight it.

> *If at first you don't succeed, remove all evidence you*
> *ever tried.*
> DAVID BRENT, *regional manager* WERNHAM HOGG
> *The Office*

WHAT HIERARCHY PROTECTS AND OBSCURES

David Brent, the "hero" of the BBC series *The Office,* is a burlesque of the worst leaders we've experienced. However, the series became an international phenomenon precisely because his antics are all too familiar to anyone who has worked in an organization of any kind. The show allows most of us to think, "At least I'm not *that* bad." Still, we're all subject to the dangers of rank and privilege. Anyone who has served in a leadership capacity, especially at the senior level, knows the familiar sense of impending hazard that comes with the job. At any given moment, negative press, prying analysts, a rival department, a demanding boss, a suspicious board member, an angry customer, an opportunistic shareholder, a technological snafu, or a miscalculated earnings report can intrude on your sense of well-being, totally unannounced and with great force. At that moment, the reality of being onstage and exposed is as real as it gets. All eyes are on you. Everyone expects a brilliant explanation and swift response. Who wouldn't find someplace to hide? When we're called on the carpet, we naturally want to fall back on the handiest excuse, or lie, or blame a scapegoat, or spout tough-sounding rhetoric, or run for the nearest restroom stall. The more power one has, the more sophisticated and well-resourced one's hiding mechanisms can be.

Don't get me wrong. I take no issue with the perquisites that accompany highly demanding, often unforgiving jobs. And some of these *should* accompany such a job's high-stakes requirements and risks. The problem is, when *privilege* becomes *protection,* and relationship is impaired, rank becomes an impediment to performance instead of a facilitator of it. It erodes the trust of others. Among followers, it breeds resentment of the leaders and distracts from the work at hand. Perhaps most significant, it brings the integrity of the leader into question when her actions and words don't match. One emerging leader told us the story of frozen salaries and cutbacks being made in her organization while the CEO received raises and bonuses. She was "stunned that so many would perceive this CEO as an effective leader while betrayal and mistrust ran rampant throughout the organization." Having privilege is one thing. Hiding behind it is something entirely different.

This type of hiding leads to a secondary problem. It obscures a leader's visibility into the organization. One CEO told us that his head of HR informed him that they indeed were "in trouble" because of a lack of real succession planning throughout the organization, and as a consequence they lacked a sufficient pipeline of leaders prepared to assume broader roles as they pursued exponential growth. The CEO was skeptical of the diagnosis. His conclusion was not that there weren't any leaders, but rather that their corporate ivory tower obscured the visibility of those leaders. He said the solution wasn't to go and hire more leaders, but rather to create the necessary visibility to see the leaders they already had. That meant they had to get out of headquarters and out into the field to meet those leaders, learn from them, and give them exposure to the broader organization, and to allow the organization to see them. To do so required a forfeiture of corporate privilege. To have "summoned" them to headquarters would have defeated the purpose. Instead, the CEO chose to put rank aside and momentarily collapse hierarchy to create access to the rest of the organization.

Let's go back for a moment to the leader who complained about the price of his watch in front of his staff. Think of what it would have meant for him to have said to the woman planning her New Jersey vacation, "I hope you have a fantastic time with your family. The Jersey shore has some of the most beautiful beaches in the country." That would have exposed his humanity as her peer. It would have required stepping off the perch of rank, stepping into her world, and participating in it well. And what is the cost of missing this opportunity? Is her resentment and shame going to do much for her productivity that day? How might she have left the meeting had he been gracious to her?

What is it that can be so intimidating, sometimes terrifying, to leaders presented with the opportunity to step off the pedestal of privilege and level the playing field with those they work?

> *These days, everyone wants John Lennon's sunglasses,*
> *accent and swagger, but no one is prepared to take their*
> *clothes off and stand naked like he did in his songs.*
> BONO, *international rock star*
> *and political activist*

THE RISK OF EXPOSURE

Conventional management wisdom has taught us for decades that keeping one's distance from others, especially those one leads, is essential to good leadership. To be objective, one mustn't get too close. By keeping that distance, the leader would ensure that her ability to make decisions about others, especially tough decisions, would never be compromised. Imagine having to deliver tough performance feedback to—or, worse, having to fire—someone who reported to you with whom you also have a close relationship.

Maybe this is even someone who had helped you in your own career. Maybe this is someone you see socially—your kids play with this person's kids, you play golf together, you enjoy each other's company—and now you have to let that person go. How can you do it without feeling guilty and loathing yourself? What happens if you can't bring yourself to do what you know you must? It's easy to see how the notion of distancing oneself from those we lead became fundamental to management acumen.

Here's the problem, though. The further a leader is from those she leads, the less reliable information she will have to be able to know what is really important to others, what their passions are, what their concerns are, and what they really believe about key decisions. Moreover, emotional distance creates the need to fill in interactions with an artificial cohesion to cover underlying feelings of uncertainty just beneath the surface. We'll talk more about that in the next couple of chapters.

And what about the myth of objectivity? Does distance really lead to it? I would suggest just the contrary. I would argue that the *more* data a leader has about those she leads, the more *genuinely objective* she can be. And when it comes time to make hard decisions and deliver bad news, it will be done from a place of care and regard, not cold, obligatory management. It appears that leaders who experience the most satisfying relationships with those they lead clearly indicate that having the confidence, trust, and access to one another enhances performance.

So why does the notion of being accessible and close to others cause many leaders fear? Because many leaders still have yet to learn that the exposure of their humanity and even their failures buys them *more* credibility, not less. Despite all that has been written on the need to be authentic, honest, and candid about our shortfalls, this becomes progressively more difficult the higher you go in an organization. The superhuman, superhero status that's either assumed by leaders or forced on them by circumstances makes the risk of exposure too great. A whole choir of today's leaders is singing the same refrain:

- "Most people I know don't think about my frailties or insecurities—even though I'm fairly open about them. I don't really believe that they get it. Still, I fear that if I appear unsure about certain things, that would compromise my leadership. So, I tend to play it safe . . ."

- "I fear the betrayal that will inevitably come when I tell the truth about my organization to my organization. The truth triggers the fears in others—especially if those folks are going to lose some measure of control. It's an ache that controls me more than I would like . . ."

- "I have worried that my job could be in danger if I showed who I really am. My fears have overcome me to the point where I wonder if the fight was really worth it . . ."

This is just a sampling of what I've heard from hundreds of account managers, junior executives, vice presidents, and pastors. It's a difficult tune to hear. The good news is that they remain open to a different kind of relationship than the one they know now. Even better, they are teaching us the tune that will captivate them. We must be willing to learn to sing in a different key.

> *When I'm riding in my limo I won't look out the window*
> *Might make me homesick for humanity*
> *There's nowhere that I can't go and there's nobody I*
>   *don't know*
> *And there's an emptiness that's eating me*
>   BARENAKED LADIES
>   *"Celebrity"*

THE PARADOX OF EXPOSURE

When was the last time you withdrew your respect from a leader who humbly accepted responsibility for a mistake? Aren't we more likely to offer greater respect and support to a leader who steps out from behind his rank to show us a human face? And with greater trust, are we not more likely to achieve greater speed? Things always move faster when we aren't second-guessing those with whom we lead.

The other side of this equation is also true. When leaders are willing to expose what they are normally inclined to hide, they set an example that invites others to do the same. So instead of all the wasted time and lost productivity that comes from shifting blame and accountability, sifting information and softening the blow of bad news, a level playing field allows for even the toughest issues to be surfaced and resolved in a fraction of the time it might otherwise take when everyone is too busy trying to run from a problem, avoid an angry boss, or avoid looking bad in front of the organization.

What makes the notion of such an environment so utterly foreign to so many, yet at the same time so desperately desired? Our inherent desire to be seen well and only well. Who among us would say we enjoy the idea of what might appear to be public humiliation and shame? Not many. So the paradox to be managed is this: *when we seek to be seen without flaws, we wind up looking untrustworthy and underperforming*. When we allow ourselves to be seen with limitations, we look trustworthy and competent. Dr. Dan Allender, in his book *Leading with a Limp*, offers this thought:

"The shadows of deceit grow in an organization where leaders hide in order to survive. The result of hiding is a labyrinth-like litany of half-truths, truths, and lies that eventually make the community cynical and mean. The mission of the organization is lost in the fury of fighting to keep power and avoid being harmed . . . Becoming a more human leader involves confessing one's need for others. To confess that I need you—to help me think through a decision or to hear my struggles—is to admit that I am not enough, period."

As I said earlier, incumbent leaders are desperate to stop carrying the weight of Herculean demands on their shoulders, self-imposed or not. It is also true that emerging leaders, who are far more naturally comfortable with vulnerability, are desperate to experience it from leaders preparing them for future leadership. Listen to what these emerging leaders told us about how they long for their leaders to be human instead of superhuman. They don't want to be led by a faux Hercules. They do want strength, but they want grace and passion as well.

- "The most remarkable leader I have seen in action was a president of an organization with eighty passionate, intelligent, diverse members. Watching her mediate, encourage, reward, and discipline was fascinating—far more fascinating than watching her manage a project."

- "I am grateful that I can confide in my boss—that she understands what I am up against. Without her, my job would be impossible. She can play the game—and she teaches me how to play. I abhor people in high positions who are there just to win the game for themselves."

Emerging leaders are developing a healthy contempt for the "ends justify the means" mentality and are demanding that their leaders respect them as participants in the process. The good news is that there are a growing number of incumbent leaders who are indeed mere mortals—and emerging leaders are thrilled to work for them.

> *Weak is the new strong.*
> ANDREW, *age twenty-eight, an emerging leader*

HOW EXPOSURE INCREASES TRUST AND CREDIBILITY

Trust based purely on position is typically short-lived. If a leader must use rank to get things done, performance is eventually going to lag—severely. Credibility is never established by rank. It might be partially established by a performance track record that takes the leader up the career ladder to increasingly broader positions. But once she reaches a new level, the track-record meter is usually reset to zero and she must start building her next portfolio of accomplishments. The only sustainable source of credibility that increases over time and changed roles is your ability to establish relationships that transcend the boundaries of rank. Your peers have odd ways of remembering what you were like, once you find your way into roles above them. Your equity with them will rise or fall not because you rise, but because they don't perceive you as treating them with any less respect *because* you rose.

A classic example of how pulling rank can lead to demise came during one of the most painful experiences of my career. I was appointed as a vice president of a department in a large division of a global corporation. The man who hired me was clearly a gifted leader, one I believed I could learn from and enjoy working with. For the sake of anonymity, let's call him "Steve." Steve appointed several VPs to key positions to help him create significant change in the organization. After about a year working with this new team, Steve's boss moved on and Steve was promoted into the vacated corporate job. Our team was suddenly without a leader and we were all highly anxious about who might fill his former role. For a handful of reasons, none of us wanted the position, and it stayed vacant for seven months. We began to hope it might just stay that way, or that we'd all get invited to be on Steve's global corporate staff. Our hope ran out when Steve's former boss, who had failed miserably in his new venture, returned and, due to his political capital, was hired into Steve's former division role. Essentially, the two men had swapped jobs. Despite our pleading with Steve to see the impending disaster on the horizon, he didn't anticipate the blind ambition that would motivate his former boss to reclaim his corporate job with a vengeance. After systematically dismantling everything that Steve had accomplished in his absence, our new boss publicly discredited each of us and fired us one by one on a whim. Steve was powerless to help within the corporate culture, and as a result he had no choice but to resign from the corporation because of the unconscionable actions of a man, who of course, ended up getting his old job back.

The drunkenness that can come from exploiting one's rank often ends in tragedy: a loss of control and, ultimately, a loss of the very influence sought in the first place. Steve's former boss, turned employee, turned replacement, finally used up all his credibility within the organization—his power rampage and the ensuing wake of bodies that accompanied it had played out for all to see. The performance of his organization became so poor, turnover so high, and litigation against him so prevalent, that the CEO had no choice but to remove him from the organization.

Now, let me offer two contrasting stories that show the supreme value of using rank in the context of meaningful relationships. The first is the story of Jim Sinegal, the CEO of Costco, who is the perfect opposite of the stereotypical high-rolling CEO. Costco is the top warehouse retailer in the United States, and its share performance is impressive, racking up a 354 percent increase in the past ten years compared with only 237 percent for the S&P 500. Costco's sales have grown 11.7 percent annually over the past five years, and its earnings have climbed 13.2 percent per year in the same period. However, when Sinegal has a meeting with a visitor at the company's headquarters in Issaquah, Washington, he goes down to the lobby himself to escort the guest to his fourth-floor office. He answers his own phone, doesn't have an executive washroom, makes do with twenty-year-old furniture, and doesn't even have an office with walls. As Sinegal puts it, "We're low-cost operators, and it would be a little phony if we tried to pretend that we're not and had all the trappings." Instead of amassing perks for himself, Sinegal focuses on boosting salaries and benefits for Costco cashiers. Despite grumblings from Wall Street analysts who think ever higher shareholder return could be achieved by holding payroll expenses down, Sinegal says, "If you hire good people, give them good jobs, and pay them good wages, generally something good is going to happen."

Here's the second story. Several years ago I was working with a CEO of a major healthcare system. The board had been pressuring him to drive revenue, given that they'd done several key acquisitions to increase their patient volumes through cross-service-line referrals. But growth was slow, costs were rising, margins were shrinking, and nobody could see where the revenue was hemorrhaging from. The CEO contemplated going before the board, at the advice of his COO, and presenting a highly spun story about how things were getting under control, how clinical and financial data were soon to be more easily accessible, and how relationships among service-line physicians were improving enough that referrals across in-patient and out-patient care volumes would soon be rising.

The problem was that these claims weren't true, and he knew it. We strongly urged him not to spin a story to the board that he'd later regret, encouraging him to simply tell the truth: that he needed time to get to the bottom of the issue, and that was going to mean changing out some key players who'd not been getting the results they'd promised. This CEO was highly conflict-averse and not easily inclined to exert his will. Nonetheless, he told the board the truth about being frustrated, gave them some plausible hunches about where the issues likely resided, and asked for three months to come back to them with a clear plan. To his surprise they were quite gracious, empathetic with his frustrations, appreciative of his candor, and supportive of the tough moves he felt he needed to make. Three months later, it was very clear that the issues resided in two major units—major surgery and oncology. The controller had been mistakenly reporting delayed volume reports, and poor scheduling in the central scheduling department for surgery had surgeons taking their patients elsewhere. Within nine months of identifying the real issues, performance was turned around, volumes were on the rise again, and clinical and financial data were being reported accurately. By disclosing his own frustrations and the truth about performance, the CEO gained credibility in the eyes of key constituents, and resolved the problems far faster than he would have had he chosen to mask them behind a charade of embellished information on the bet that he wouldn't get caught.

In both of these examples, we see CEOs who behave like regular, fallible people trying to do their best for their employees, their shareholders, and their companies. The trappings of rank and privilege aren't influencing what these leaders are doing—their motivator is trying to find out what's *right* and acting on it. I am daily confronted by leaders who have a desperate urge to spin information and shape perceptions that run counter to the truth. It takes enormous courage and humility to use rank judiciously. Anyone can use their influential position to self-protect and hide. But the wake of cynicism from decades of such behavior has left emerging leaders intolerant and incumbent leaders all guilty by association.

For the Moment

How would others say you have used rank?

Have there been consequences that were desirable?

Would others use the words *courageous* and *humble* to describe you?

PRIVILEGE AND RANK: DIFFERENT MEANINGS TO DIFFERENT LEADERS

One of the classic definitions of leadership offered during the 1980s was *The art of getting others to want to do things you are convinced should be done.* At the time, the definition seemed insightful and inspirational. Trainers and professors would dissect the definition, focusing on the abstraction of *art,* the importance of desire in *to want,* and the phrase *you are convinced* with its emphasis on the importance of conviction in leaders. All noble and good. But nobody ever spent time on the *getting others* part. In hindsight, that required more attention. Because *getting* has come to mean a broad range of approaches, regardless of the consequence. As we'll explore in Chapter Four, the *getting others to want to* part has come more to mean *to make them think it's their idea.* And the *should be done* part has mushroomed into a dogged results orientation, often disregarding the consequences. For many incumbent leaders, successful leadership has been about the ends, not the means. Despite much attention drawn to the process of leadership, organizations of all kinds still measure their success by outcome.

Hear me well—results are important, and exceeding expectations of achievement ought to be celebrated. But the power surge accompanying that achievement includes an emotional invoice, and too frequently others are asked to pay it. The addiction to those surges can cause leaders to *get others to do things* at all costs—ethics, life balance, manipulation, coercion, and exhaustion. Intended consequences? Of course not. To most, the pursuit of lofty objectives and the ensuing pride in accomplishment more than justifies whatever it takes to get those results. Emerging leaders are simply far more scrutinizing of the cost of those results than most incumbent leaders ever needed to be.

The concept of *followership* used to be a respected concept—denoting the status of a disciple or advocate for a leader as an avid supporter of his vision and direction. But in the complexity of a global and technology-driven economy, this kind of *followership* must simply die. What leaders need now is many others leading with them. Not *under* them. Not *for* them. Not *following* them. But *leading with* them.

Unfortunately, *follower* has come to mean *spectator.* Tenacious would-be leaders come to know the cues of a leader who has set off on a course from which he has no interest in deviating. No need to follow with conviction; just go through the motions and watch the leader do his thing. When leadership becomes a solo act, don't waste time looking around for others to energetically get on board. Ira Chaleff, in his wonderful book *The Courageous Follower,* says it so well:

"Dynamic leaders are the spark, the flame that ignites action. With vision, they generate and focus power. But followers are the guarantors of the beneficial use of power. Dynamic leaders may use power well, but they cannot be the guarantors. In their passion, their expansiveness, their drive, dynamic leaders are prone to excess: a deal too large, a bottom line too important, a cause too righteous, an image too pure, a lifestyle too rich, an enemy too hated, a bridge too far."

Unfortunately, to the emerging leader, high rank has become nearly synonymous with corruption, conspiracy, and arrogance. Emerging leaders grew up in the post-1960s era of Watergate, gained isolated independence as latchkey kids, and learned to be cynical during the energy crisis. They don't remember the Kennedy White House, but they do remember—and many of them believe—Oliver Stone's *JFK*. They've grown up believing that the old ways of defined pecking order, strict hierarchy, and slow pro-motional tracks are misguided and inefficient. They are skeptical about what they're told. They need feedback and flexibility, but despise close supervision. They believe their merit has already earned them a rightful place of importance, and they yearn—or demand—to be treated as peers. Their distrust of those in author-ity has led them to desire unrealistic degrees of egalitarianism as a misguided way to avoid the abuse of power.

At the extreme, emerging leaders often believe rank shouldn't be seen or heard. They struggle to reconcile the need for direction and clarity with having another's will imposed on them. Their im-pulse to reject rank is strong, particularly when being forced to defer to another's views equates with tacit endorsement of those views. Despite this impulse, they understand that a perpetual stale-mate will result in nothing getting done. Even if they are ready to acknowledge that hierarchy is good if used properly, they're not sure they know what that looks like. As one emerging leader put it, "We are witnessing first hand the behind-the-scenes hypocrisy, and learning that in leadership roles it's only a matter of time before 'being liked' and 'doing the right thing' come into con-flict." Emerging leaders earnestly want to believe in their leaders, but they're plagued by their experience of rank-hoarding leaders. One emerging leader told us, "My boss thinks his title grants him limitless power over everyone."

Balance lies somewhere between the exertion of complete authority accorded one's rank and the abandonment of exercising any influence on the other—a dynamic in constant flux. In the degree to which a leader exerts her will and the degree to which, *in the same moment,* she can look into the eyes of those she leads and express both her hopes and uncertainty about her will—that is where the balance is beautifully struck.

Rank—inasmuch as it consists of the clarifying of one's role and the exercise of influence toward generative outcomes—is good. Being a leader of influence and using the authority accorded with one's position, in the service of moving an organization forward, is very good. Leadership should never be about only one person getting their way at the expense of others. Nor is leadership ever about everyone getting their way. It is a paradox—leaders must use their position well in the service of a strategic intent, but in doing so they will inevitably both inspire and infuriate with the same action. This reality is painful for both leaders who must cause the tension and leaders who must live with the tension.

The tension of hierarchy is complex. Rank does have privileges. Sometimes those privileges are unfair, and sometimes we're just envious of them. And rank also comes with significant cost. My clients often tell me how pained they are by the isolation of their role. They long for the moments of camaraderie with true colleagues, yet are paralyzed by the political implications of letting down their guard. Ironically, it is in the letting down of their guard that their influence can either become secured or be taken advantage of. Benevolent leaders who forfeit the protection of rank to make themselves vulnerable are often trampled by the opportunism of others' selfish ambitions. In their hurt, they return to their hiding place of rank. Both emerging and incumbent leaders resent this.

Incumbent leaders who have the courage to exert influence in the service of helping an organization flourish, even in the face of disappointing others, are a needed asset. And emerging leaders who have the desire to ensure that authority is used justly, even if it means decisions might be slower and outcomes might take longer, are also a needed asset. We need to learn to embrace both views as complementary rather than opposing. Not all incumbent leaders are benevolent dictators or, worse, harmful despots, self-servingly presiding over others. And not all emerging leaders are recalcitrant rebels, intent on overthrowing any authority that dares constrain their free expression. It is sad that each often experiences the other that way.

I believe more incumbent leaders than not want to lead justly, use authority humbly, and, to the best of their ability, ensure that the privileges of their rank never harm others or provide a shelter behind which to hide. And I believe more emerging leaders than not are yearning to use influence well, yet fear having no one to show them how. I believe behind their jaded eyes are hopeful hearts and a belief they can change the world if given the chance. And indeed they will. Together, incumbent and emerging leaders could join forces and create new authority structures that neither has ever experienced, yet in which both could thrive in ways not possible alone. Here are some starter thoughts on how to do that.

The Bridge to Relationship: Neutralizing Rank to Accelerate Trust and Performance

The ultimate cost of abused rank is losing the trust of those from whom we most need it. Without their trust, we will never have their best thinking or contribution. The most effective way to offset that potential drain of trust is through exposing our vulnerability. I hope these ideas, many of which came from the leaders in our research, offer some guidance as you find ways to build relationships with leaders around you. Undoubtedly you will have many other ideas to add to the list.

1. *Negotiate clear boundaries.* One of the simplest issues leaders often overlook is the need to be clear about what they expect of one another. I tell my clients to "lead out loud" often, especially when a relationship is new. Political dynamics and strenuous performance pressures cause others to attach meaning to nearly everything a leader says—and, even more so, what a leader *doesn't* say. Leaders can never presume the boundary conditions for authority are clear. Talk openly about how specific decisions will be made and actions will get taken and what role people will play in which

decisions. When you have made decisions, let people know the rationale behind them so they don't misinterpret your reasoning. If you sense people feel dissatisfied about their authority levels, ask them to talk about it. It doesn't mean you will alter your decision, but it does mean you will have heard their concerns.

2. *Never forget that privileges you enjoy might trouble others.* This doesn't mean it's about you; it might simply be the envy of others. But if you sense resentment over the privileges you have been afforded, or you have inadvertently signaled a high level of enjoyment of those privileges, others may ascribe self-seeking motives for your being in your job. Once others have concluded that you are self-serving, everything you do becomes evidence to support that conclusion. You may never understand the cold shoulders you receive from others, but it could have to do with how you have enjoyed the privileges that come with your role. You will never alleviate this completely in an organization, nor should you try, especially from those who observe you from a distance. But for the key relationships with those whom you regularly interact, you should be diligent about knowing how they experience your treatment of privilege.

3. *Generously share the privileges; never gloat.* It may sound ridiculously simply, but when you get to enjoy nice meals at restaurants, while others have to eat at the deli or bring leftovers from home, people notice. Take others to lunch. This is not to pity them or to treat them as the underprivileged getting a taste of the good life—doing so looks like you're subtly trying to rub their nose in your privilege. Be gracious, and invite others to partake in some of the benefits of your role. Include those at different places on the hierarchy. I've heard dozens of stories from CEOs who will routinely schedule lunches and dinners with people from all over the organization, and the level of appreciation and respect it garners them is enormous, not to mention the value of the conversation that gives leaders access to views and perspectives they'd otherwise never hear. You should scrupulously avoid ever talking about anything to do with your financial status, your personal possessions, the convenience of riding on the corporate jet, or the cost of your daughter's wedding or your recent vacation, and you should never get sucked into such conversation by someone looking to one-up

others. You should, in fact, strongly discourage such conversation. It breeds resentment and is really in poor taste.

4. *Expose the struggles that accompany rank.* This is *not* a license to whine or complain all the time. We all have been around leaders who feel the need to continuously talk about how exhausted they are, how late they were up doing emails, how early they started their day, how much work they did on the weekend, and so on. But the fact is, the demands on leaders are unique and consuming, often depleting, and although others can't be in your shoes, your sharing with them what that sometimes feels like can go a long way toward demystifying the alleged grandeur of power. Making your humanity visible in the context of privilege is one of your greatest assets toward building trust, which is the fundamental building block of speed. Don't hide it.

5. *Stop resenting or judging others for their influence.* It's so convenient to lump all leaders, especially incumbent leaders, into the category of "opportunistic post-Enron, greedy autocrats." Truth is, most aren't. But if you judge and convict them all before you even know them, you will miss incredible opportunities for relationships that can be transformative. Pay close attention to your own biases about authority, and watch out for the ease with which you can subconsciously project those onto others. If a leader displays confidence, be grateful for that confidence, and don't assume it means anything more. If a leader makes a decision, don't instantly conclude they have deliberately thwarted you. Instead, engage them in conversation, even if that feels risky. Your candor is welcomed more often than you think it is. Your resentment and judgment, or a perpetual instinct to be rebellious, only fuel your fellow leaders' impulse to withdraw and hide and to exert their will more forcefully. Your graciousness, by contrast, invites a more open stance, a willingness to risk exposure, and an exercise of authority that is both strong and kind.

6. *Create access to the organization.* Nothing will completely prevent obscured visibility into the organization, but you can take deliberate action to ensure you have the greatest possible lines of sight. Be sure you create mechanisms that get you off of any hierarchical perch and out into your organization—anywhere the action is. Plants, stores, laboratories, distribution centers, call centers, and

field offices are places where people need to see you, and where you will get your best access to, and view of, those desperately desiring to be seen by you. Ask genuinely curious questions of those you meet with, and take the time to hear their stories. Allow them to ask you no-holds-barred questions about your role and what you are working on. These conversations, on their turf, will go a long way toward neutralizing hierarchy.

7. *Extend trust before it is earned.* One of the ways to ensure that trust is established, especially from those not inclined to extend it, is to offer it from the get-go. By inviting people into your circle, you convey to them that you trust them—no strings attached. It leaves them the option to reciprocate or not, but at least they have a more accurate view of who they are extending trust to or withholding it from. Conversely, by keeping your distance you risk reinforcing potentially inaccurate conclusions about your trustworthiness and, worse, you fortify the use of erroneous criteria others might be using to assess your, and others', trustworthiness.

So let's check in on Nancy and Don. It would be easy to assume the conversation they were about to have would end unpleasantly for one or both of them, especially Don. There would likely be an apparent winner and loser, but in reality, both would lose. One day soon, I hope for tough conversations like that to play out something like this . . .

> Nancy shut the door to Don's office as he took a seat behind his desk. She took a deep breath, then sat in the chair across from him. They stared at each other in perplexity, both knowing the tension between them, yet both accepting that underneath they had a strong mutual respect for each other's talent and insight.

> The awkwardness of the silence got to Nancy first, so she jumped in. "Don, I gotta tell you, there are just days I don't know what to make of you. Most days, your brilliance blows me away. You have more talent and knowledge of Brookreme than most people who've been here twice as long as you have, and you have what seems to be bottomless energy. But there are other days you just frustrate the hell out of me, and you already know today is one of those days."

> Don did a good job not letting Nancy see him gulp, and he worked to remain calm though his anxiety was rising. He was certain the next sentence was

going to signal his being jettisoned from Brookreme. Still, he couldn't resist the impulse to defend himself. "Well, Nancy, I guess that makes two of us," he said. "I get that you are the boss and you get to have your way, but when you make decisions that I think don't make any sense, I just go nuts. I know you are wickedly smart, and I jumped at the chance to report to you because I knew I'd learn a ton from you. And I have. But sometimes it feels like you are just a bully."

Now Nancy's blood was boiling. She felt Don was being disrespectful and arrogant. But she had sworn to herself she would take Jim's advice. Careful to keep her voice at a conversational level, she said, "I get that there are times you don't like directions I choose, Don. But can you honestly say that you don't feel like you have influenced me at all? Your fingerprints are all over the direction of this company, and your input has shaped countless numbers of my decisions. Do you honestly expect that every decision will go your way?"

Without missing a beat, Don leaned forward on his desk and retorted, "But why didn't you tell me before the meeting today that you'd planned to go in the opposite direction? You asked me to do all kinds of thinking about Europe, you knew that I thought Asia was a sinkhole, and yet you never closed the loop. I had to find out in the middle of the room in front of everybody else. Couldn't you have at least had the courtesy to come back and let me know so I wasn't blindsided in front of the whole team?"

"Well to be honest, I just didn't want to have another debate with you," Nancy replied. "I knew you'd be frustrated, and frankly, Don, sometimes I just don't have the energy to explain everything over and over. But I can see how today would have felt disrespectful to your work, so I can own that. I'm sorry."

That stopped Don cold. He'd never heard Nancy apologize. After a moment, he said, "Wow. I've never heard you say that." His need to keep fighting faded.

"Don, I'm human too," Nancy said. "I have to balance a lot of people's ideas and needs, but at the end of the day, I'm accountable to a lot of people for the results of this place. And they put me in this role because I have experience and have been successful more than I've failed. Yes, I've had some miserable failures. But I'm not stupid. And sometimes I just need you to trust me, even if you disagree. And when you do disagree, I don't need you pouting and huffing like a child when you are around the executive team. They respect you, but you know that I advocated hard for you to get this role against some of their feelings about your inexperience. You can't keep reinforcing some of their beliefs that you are just an immature, ivy-league snot who thinks he's hot stuff. I know you are more than that. But you have to show me, and the organization, that you are as well."

"Well, I know I can be a hothead sometimes," Don admitted. "Drives my wife crazy. I just get excited about new ideas, so I don't know how to deal with it when I hit a wall. So I get pissed. I'll work on it."

"So will I have your support on moving ahead with China?"

"I'll give it my all. Just next time keep me in the loop, OK?"

"Got it. I'll work on that," Nancy said.

The conversation ended with Brookreme's characteristic soft high five and a knowing grin that spoke volumes on each of their faces. They knew something important had just happened, and they also knew it wouldn't be the last time the two of them would pit wills against one another. There was an unspoken, newfound respect between them that made the inevitable next time more a chance to intellectually spar with a good colleague and mentor than just another exhausting opportunity to battle over turf.

For the Moments Yet to Come . . .

1. How have your beliefs about rank been shaped?
2. What do you like most and least about using the influence that comes with your role?
3. How do you manage the privileges of your rank? Of others' rank?
4. How would your organization see faster results and greater trust if the negative effects of hierarchy were eliminated?

CHAPTER TWO

A GREAT CUP OF COFFEE

The Death of Veneer, The Dare of Depth

I have measured out my life with coffee spoons.

T. S. Eliot

Opportunity: Have deeper conversations, not better transactions, to surface innovative and dangerous thinking.

Is this you?

> "OK, everyone, let's take a quick fifteen-minute break, and when we come back, we'll start the next section on slide two-thirty-two. I know this might feel a bit tedious, but we're making good progress. We have only two hours left, so we'll need to pick up the pace if we're going to get through the whole deck."

The speaker was Al, Brookreme's strategic planning manager of many years. Al had always assumed that his seniority and back-to-front knowledge of Brookreme and its markets would guarantee him, in time, the top strategy position in the company. When Nancy promoted Don to head of strategy, it had been a huge pill for Al to swallow. Al had overcompensated by producing incredibly detailed analytics—it appeared that he could tell you precisely how many angels were dancing on the head of a pin. Al hadn't noticed just how far overboard he had gone, though. The results were the most notoriously mind-numbing meetings in the company. Al seemed blithely unaware of all the rolling eyes as his colleagues fled gasping for the restrooms, the coffeepot, their offices, anyplace to get out of his interminable meetings. Ironically, Al's stellar analytical capability and his interpersonal tone-deafness were what had led to his being passed over for the long-awaited promotion in the first place. He was simultaneously too good with the data and too unable to interact strategically with his fellow executives.

People tolerated Al because he was—all things considered—a very kind-hearted, friendly guy. People also frankly assumed that he'd be retiring in the near future. But Al seemed bent on staying there, despite being passed over, and his colleagues were beginning to wonder if he planned on staying with Brookreme long after they had all moved on.

It had been nearly three months since Don's department had embarked on blazing the trail into the Pacific Rim. Don had asked Al to lead a trio of studies—market research, competition, and customer needs. Al had been commissioned to sift this data and help Brookreme land on the best approach to effectively penetrate such a vast, untapped and untested market. With yet another one of Al's legendary presentations running into triple overtime, Don found himself cornered in the hallway by Brookreme's COO, Jim.

"Don, I've just got to ask. When are you gonna deal with the way Al presents this stuff?" With a look of pain on his face, Jim continued, "Everyone is in there nodding their heads at heaven only knows what, and we're all too fried after slide eighty to know what questions to ask. The thing is, when we all fall asleep, Al just rambles on and on. We've been in there now for almost five hours! I don't even have a clue what Al thinks we should do. Do you?"

Don tried to calm Jim down. "I know it's a lot of data, Jim, but I'm on it. That's exactly why I didn't have Nancy come to this session. I've got to give Al the chance to get through all the gory details, and then I'll summarize it all for the management committee. I'm sure some people are feeling a bit over-whelmed, but this is really important information and people need to know what this is gonna take from each of them to make it work."

Don's explanation only seemed to irritate Jim more. "Who gives a crap about Nancy and the management committee?" he exclaimed. "Do you think for one minute anyone in there is getting *anything*? Most of them are scared to death that we're gonna stick them on a plane to Shanghai tomorrow to go launch a new venture and all they've got to work with is a pile of charts and graphs that don't make sense to anyone but Al. Now we've got two hours left in there. I suggest you figure out how to help him not make this a forced march through the last two tabs of his tome. Help Al get some of the real questions on the table. That's what everyone is desperately scrambling to figure out. Al's information might be theoretically brilliant in some way, Don, but it doesn't do anyone any damn good if people walk out of that room at the end of today like deer in headlights. We're betting the entire Pacific Rim strategy on their knowing what we expect them to do."

Don's first impulse was to fight back and remind Jim he wasn't his boss. But he knew in his gut Jim was trying to be helpful, and, even more fundamentally, Don knew Jim was right. Jim had been a great COO; he had watched out for Don since he joined the management committee. He had been there for Don several times in stressful moments with Nancy. Don was grateful for that, and he knew Jim was just trying to watch his back here too. He choked down his pride and asked, "So what would you suggest I ask Al to do with the last section of the meeting? He's done all this work. I don't want him to feel like we're throwing it all back in his face. We all know how sensitive he can get about his deliverables."

Jim paused, slightly surprised by Don's question. Frankly, he'd expected a defensive argument. After a moment, Jim said, "Well, I think you need to assume that Al wants Brookreme to succeed in Asia more than he wants a pat on the back for his work. If you start with that assumption, you can probably help him see that, even with brilliant data, he's not heading down that path. And worse, he might be unknowingly setting folks up to fail. Of course he's not gonna like hearing it, but what's the alternative, Don? If people walk out of the room today *less* confident in what they need to do, what do you think will happen? It will be Toronto all over again!" Jim knew that dig would sting, but he wanted to make sure Don really understood his point.

It worked.

Don winced and shut his eyes for a moment. He remembered six years earlier, when he was just an analyst, as if it were yesterday. Brookreme had tried to move into the Toronto market with a team that showed up green and unprepared. They got slaughtered in the market. It took three years to recover the losses and turn a profit there. But the feasibility studies—*Al's studies*—all had suggested they'd have black ink inside a year. The data were accurate; the execution was fumbled by a well-intended but unprepared team who never admitted their fears until the postmortem at the end of the first year when it came time to find a scapegoat. Al escaped unscathed, and the sales executive took the bullet. Don could vividly see Jim's prophecy coming true, but the bloodbath would be even greater if Asia tanked. Too many eyes—those of journalists, analysts, shareholders, and the board, for starters—were on this, not to mention Nancy's reputation, and maybe even her job.

"Tell everyone the break will be about half an hour long instead of just fifteen minutes," Don said. "Make something up; I don't care what. And I'll see what I can do. Thanks, Jim."

They parted and walked in opposite directions. Jim headed to where the team had gathered for a break—and to vent their frustrations—to let them know the meeting would continue in a half hour. Don walked back toward the conference room where Al was busy getting ready for the next section of the meeting. Don walked in and shut the door.

Al grinned and said, "Hey, Don! It's going really well, don't you think? Man, it's exciting to think about how this is really gonna put Brookreme on the global map! How do you think folks are doing? Seems like they're grasping this, no sweat. I've been checking around the room during the discussion, and people are nodding and seem to get it. What's your take?"

For the Moment

Does Al work at your organization?

What was your last conversation with him like?

In what ways is your organization (not) a safe place to tell or hear the honest truth?

If you're Don, what's your opening line to Al?

We've all been in these meetings. We've all suffered through agonizingly long, boringly tedious presentations that had to be divided into two binders because they wouldn't fit into one, and spent days locked in stifling, windowless conference rooms under the pretense of a discussion about the future direction of our organization. Why do leaders insist on paralyzing people's ability to have meaningful conversation by structuring interactions that accomplish little more than staged dramatic monologues at the expense of any dialogue?

Beats me. But as a consultant, I've worked for years trying to aim my clients away from such behavior. "Death by PowerPoint Poisoning" has become one of Dilbert's best-known comics for a reason. This has nothing to do with the Microsoft software—it's great software. It's how the software is being used that's the problem. What was intended to *foster* meaningful conversation has become a weapon to *kill* meaningful conversation. Patrick Lencioni, in his fun book *Death by Meeting,* sums it up well:

"Most of us hate meetings. We complain about, try to avoid, and long for the end of meetings, even when we're running them! How pathetic is it that we have come to accept that the activity most central to running our organizations is inherently painful and unproductive? . . . If we hate meetings, can we be making good decisions and successfully leading our organizations? . . . The hard truth is, bad meetings almost always lead to bad decisions, which is the best recipe for mediocrity."

> *CONVERSATION, n. A fair for the display of minor mental commodities, each exhibitor being too intent upon the arrangement of his own wares to observe those of his neighbor.*
> AMBROSE BIERCE, *American satirist*

THE DANGER OF CONVERSATION

At Mars Hill Graduate School, where I serve as chief operating officer as well as professor of leadership, the metaphor that is used to describe the art of meaningful, high-impact conversation is *having a great cup of coffee.* What is often mistaken in many organizations for meaningful conversation is actually intense *discussion* or *debate.* Interestingly, the word *discussion* comes from the same derivative root as *percussion* and *concussion.* Like these words, which refer to the repeated hitting of something—a drum or one's head—most discussions in organizations today are the same: the hitting of one's point over and over until others "get it."

Why would we want to make sure we don't have meaningful conversations about where our businesses are headed? One very good reason is that in most organizations, conversation can be perilous. Annette Simmons, in her wonderful book on dialogue, *A Safe Place for Dangerous Truths,* describes this phenomenon well:

"Too many people think it is futile to speak the truth at work. They think that to be honest and authentic is to commit career suicide. . . . And so they compromise. They keep quiet about delicate issues. . . . And soon enough, subjects that are undiscussable exceed the discussable. All that is left are the inane, superficial, and repetitious details that monopolize our workplace conversations."

What evolves, then, is veneer. The depth of meaningful interaction is forfeited for a safe, plastic-coated image that exchanges pleasantries in public—and truth in private. The amount of wasted energy and resources can be staggering. One CEO I spoke with told me his organization estimated that it spent "tens of millions of dollars on preparation of annual strategic planning presentations that never got to the heart of strategic issues." He finally banned the use of slides altogether and made all the business unit heads submit their materials a week in advance, so that the meetings were focused more on conversations about critical issues and opportunities than on the presentation of projections and assumptions. The preparation time was cut to less than half of what it had been, and the quality of conversation rose exponentially. He went on to say, "Although people were extremely uncomfortable at the beginning, after they realized that not having the answer to every question I might ask was OK, and that they could actually learn something from their peers, they realized that they could take ideas and prioritize better coming out of the session. And when their assumptions were misguided, and unforeseen risk loomed around the corner, they finally came to realize that getting help on the front end of a strategy was better than getting halfway through an initiative before realizing it."

Simmons concludes, "We need to build a safe place where these dangerous truths can surface. We need to make it okay to question, wonder, and reflect. Only then can our organizations begin to achieve the level of responsiveness and foresight necessary for long-term success. Our mills of creativity require the grist of truth telling to produce new ideas, innovative products, and ingenious short cuts to accelerate delivery times. Half-truths only inspire half-hearted efforts and mediocre results. It is the genuine exchange of meaningful truth that gives birth to enthusiasm, passion, and excellence."

Emerging leaders seem to be having a hard time finding such a safe place. Add that to the ambivalence they already feel about leadership, and it's not hard to understand why they're reluctant to share their views. Our research revealed a consistent pattern of anxiety about speaking and failing.

Some of our respondents' fears are remarkably practical. One emerging leader told us, "I worry that one of my staff will come to me with a question that I can't answer." Some of their fears are deeply personal. One young leader described walking into a meeting this way: "I feel incredibly anxious that my boss will see me 'in action' and realize that he made a mistake thinking I could be a leader." Somehow, the fear of being seen and heard, when added to the fear of being inadequate or unprepared, creates a dangerous environment in which productivity suffers. When asked about a dangerous leadership scenario, one leader ended her story this way, "My boss simply did not respect me as a human being. The only thing he cared about was getting 'it' done at all costs." I wonder what it would mean if leaders learned to resist the seduction of getting "it" done and began to realize that when the whole story gets told, the ends rarely justify the means.

THE SEDUCTION OF TRANSACTIONS

To the incumbent leader, productivity can be an addiction. The more activity one can cram into a day, the more productive one feels, and therefore the more *valuable* one feels. There is an interesting irony as I observe the demands on a CEO's or senior executive's time. In an attempt to "reach out" and have personal impact on many people, most executives are so scattered and transactional in their dealings with others that there is precious little time devoted to the cultivation of one-on-one relationships in which genuine conversation can take place. So instead of devoting time to meaningful conversations with the people most influential to advancing their agenda, many executives have many short, superficial conversations to check off the "I reached out" box on their to-do lists. In the early 1990s, a Center for Creative Leadership study showed that most leaders spent an average of nine minutes on any given problem and worked on up to two hundred distinct problems in a given week. That, of course, was before the impact of email and Internet and intranet networks hit. Most of the senior executives I work with these days average about 150 emails a day—and this is after everything personal or trivial is already weeded out. Even if an executive spends a mere two minutes, on average, dealing with each of these email messages, it would take five hours *each day* to sort through all of them.

At the same time, employees have more information at their fingertips—both officially on firm intranets and unofficially on the

Internet—about what is going on than ever before. Instead of actually having to schedule face or phone time with their boss, they can just email. Since the boss has a PDA, people pretty much expect that he has no real down time. Dozens of clients of mine respond to emails in the wee hours of the morning, on weekends, on vacation, around the clock. The result seems to be that leaders feel ever more exhausted by the maelstrom of information assailing them, yet they are able to spend less and less time actually interacting with people face to face to handle issues being raised.

Now, I'm not knocking interconnectivity and digital technologies. We can enable greater efficiencies and increase competitive advantage through advanced technologies that make information available, link everyone together, and boost output—and this is something for which we should be grateful. Today's leaders matured in the context in which those same technologies were birthed, and they are simply doing what they have been conditioned to do. And, for the most part, doing it extraordinarily well. We can see the impact of these technologies in substantial increases in productivity. For example, U.S. output per worker grew at an annual rate of 1.4 percent in the nineteen years from 1973 to 1994, but in the nine years from 1995 to 2004, U.S. output per worker grew at a 2.9 percent annual rate—and the Bureau of Labor Statistics reported productivity gains at a 3.2 percent annual rate for the first quarter of 2005 and a 2.2 percent annual rate for the second quarter. It's no coincidence that that nine-year time period corresponds exactly to the consumer launch of the Internet and widespread business adoption of email usage. It didn't matter if leaders' management style became increasingly transactional, as long as that email in-box got emptied, right?

The problem is, although today's incumbent leaders have embraced the demand to sustain a riveting focus on performance, tomorrow's leaders have not. Emerging leaders have a strong propensity toward conversations that go beyond "just the facts, please" to the exploration of underlying assumptions, beliefs, frustrations, and hopes. One emerging leader described her boss this way: "He's intelligent, quick on his feet, but most striking is the way he works with people. He focuses on others constantly. He wants to hear everyone's story to tease out the best in them." When we asked about the most valuable conversations, emerging leaders were quick to tell us about leaders who "took them seriously," "talked without agenda," "connected in a way that transcended the workplace," and "listened more and talked less." It's clear that emerging leaders want to connect with their leaders. But not at any cost. In fact, when asked if they would turn down a promotion if it meant working for a leader whose behavior was inconsistent with their own values, more than 80 percent of them said "absolutely." Not only do they want to connect and be in relationship, they will refuse to put themselves into situations that they feel might compromise their ability to do so.

The fallacy of pursuing a higher volume of effective transactions as a means to performance is this: transactions, regardless of how well they go, can erode trust instead of strengthening it. And in environments caked with suspicion, people's most innovative ideas will remain safely concealed. Transactional environments reinforce the veneer of superficiality because score is kept on volume, not depth. So one's value appears to rise and fall not on the merits of being honest, but only on what numbers one produces. The volume of activity one completes, or at least *appears* to complete, supersedes the strength of one's character. And emerging leaders have come to resent this.

Edward Marshall, author of *Building Trust at the Speed of Change*, suggests that cultures of transaction-based organizations are driven by fear:

"Behind all the slogans for teams, empowerment, quality . . . is fear . . . the fear of not measuring up to the expectations of supervisors, not being considered a top performer, or worse yet, being embarrassed in one's peer group by being excluded from projects or processes that matter. The operating premise for working in a transactional culture is to be 'nice, but not honest.' Candor is not rewarded. Conflicts are avoided or dealt with off line. The rumor mill provides a way for people to share their truths or perceptions about how the organization really works."

Such shrouded communications and fearful interactions remind me of an experience I had early in my career, when I worked in a large, global Fortune 50 retail food and beverage corporation. It was a ruthlessly competitive environment, but I wasn't savvy enough to fully detect that on the way in. I took the job because I was told it would punch my career ticket. Soon after arriving, it became painfully clear I was missing something important. In meetings, everyone would be talking in what felt like code language, and of course, I'd be the one to blurt out, "Wait, I thought we were here to talk about how to help the Detroit region deal with its production capacity issue." It was almost as if I wasn't in the room. People just kept talking in code—a code that became increasingly opaque to me as my time in the organization unfolded. When I had my first performance appraisal, my clients in the organization raved about my work. But my boss and peers had less flattering things to say, citing me as "politically naïve" and someone who "doesn't seem to know his place." And to be fair, there was probably some truth to both concerns. Taking political cues has never been my forte.

At the bottom of the appraisal form was a section titled "Sustainable Contribution." When I asked what that meant, my boss told me, "Well, since we have so much turnover here in the organization as people move through their assignments quickly, we're trying to make sure that people aren't just focused on getting their next promotion within eighteen months, but rather, making sure they make a sustainable contribution in the role they are in. We feel that getting people to focus on this in their performance planning will help them avoid the insidious face-time issue in our culture where people are only committed to looking like they are working hard instead of actually producing something of importance for the organization in which they are currently assigned." Made sense to me. At that point in the conversation, I should have quit while I was ahead. But I felt compelled to ask what seemed like an obvious question: "Don't you think there are a number of other factors that contribute to that cultural issue we should also be addressing? I'd be glad to help work on some of those as my sustainable contribution." (I was actually proud of myself for not saying what I really wanted to say, which was, "You gotta be kidding me! The people in this snake pit only know one kind of contribution—killing off their internal competitors on the way up the ladder.") Two months later I was asked if I wanted to volunteer for a severance package since corporate headquarters was cutting costs that quarter and needed to downsize. I accepted the invitation.

The Dare of Depth: The Power of Being Seen and Heard

Can you think of a time when you were in the presence of some-one you respected, someone of importance, and they entered your world and listened to what you had to say? And really heard you? How did it make you feel? Did it summon from your core a pro-found sense of significance? When you got home that evening, was there a conversation that began something like, "Honey, guess who I had a good talk with today?"

Why is it that genuine conversation with people of importance is such an affirming experience? The fact is, we are all hungry for some degree of validation. We all long to have our own significance legitimized in the eyes of those we hold in highest esteem. True, this can become excessive if dependency overshadows the experi-ence of affirmation. But for the most part, having the blessing of respect from those we respect in the form of meaningful conver-sation brings forth our best.

And here's the tragic irony of it all: we spend so much time looking for it from others that we miss offering it to those who most want it from *us*.

People in the workplace are starved for meaningful exchanges of truthful information, and they long to share their wildest ideas with people who care to listen and affirm them. Sadly, there is a real lack of honest exchanges in companies. A recent Towers Perrin sur-vey found the following disturbing statistics:

- Only 42 percent of employees believe what they're told about the company's business strategy
- Just 39 percent of employees believe that communications they receive from management about their compensation are truthful

The same report found something very interesting for our pur-poses, though: 48 percent of employees believe they receive more credible information from their direct superior than from the CEO. This study suggests that people are skeptical about what the company leadership in general tells them, but they're more will-ing to give their *immediate* leader the benefit of the doubt. Leaders who take this to heart and reach out in a personal way will find people eager to connect. And this doesn't have to take place in a formal, structured way—in fact it's better if this becomes part of a leader's informal style. It may even be the source of the leader's most legitimate power. Emerging leaders reported again and again that their most powerful conversations have been the ones that were not planned. They were the conversations that happen in pauses outside the office door and stolen moments in the break room. Incumbent leaders have lived for so long without this experience that it doesn't occur to many of them to look for it, much less provide it. Too many incumbent leaders still have an underlying assumption that people should be grateful they *have* a job. Even though the U.S. economy has transitioned from a primarily industrial economy into a predominantly services-based, knowledge economy, vestiges of a "leave your brains at the door" mentality still remain. Today's leaders remember being expected to perform the job they were hired for, without annoying their supervisors with "bright ideas." By contrast, many emerging leaders insist on being heard. To overcompensate for the "be grateful you have a job" messages they have received, many have responded with a "be grateful you have *me*" attitude. Both are postures of defense, and understandable byproducts of their respective generations. Neither serves the cause of meaningful conversation well.

One CEO told us of an annual innovation forum his corporation holds. It costs them over $500,000 to host this global event, which showcases some of the greatest innovations from around their organization. He said,

> When I was first approached about the idea, I was very skeptical. I questioned whether or not anyone would want to come, or care about what others were doing. But as I walked around the conference hall, person after person literally preened like a peacock at the opportunity to tell my team of the great work they had done, the new products they'd developed, the processes they had improved. Some told me later with tears in their eyes how proud they were to be part of our organization after seeing the incredible work of their peers. And the most powerful result was the inspiration it gave to people in other business units struggling with issues they'd seen their peers tackle. Their conclusion was "if they can do it, so can we." Today, we now do three different types of these forums annually, and they are

the best investments we could make. The cost of bringing people in from all over the world pales in comparison to the millions of dollars of performance improvement people take back with them, and the enthusiasm and passion for their organizations. But if I had not allowed the leader who pushed so hard to start such an event, I would have never known what was possible. By listening to him, I now get to listen to many in my organization I'd otherwise never get to interact with, and they get to interact with my team.

One emerging leader told this powerful story of being seen and heard in the context of a faith-based organization:

> Our leadership team met every Monday morning at 8:30. Jim, the [top leader] of the organization didn't care that I had worked all weekend. I was the youngest member of the team, and we were all expected to be at these meetings. I had been at an offsite with a number of our younger members of the organization training them that weekend. It had been an incredible experience. I showed up, bleary eyed, at the staff meeting and when it was my turn to talk, I couldn't help it, I gushed. I had been blown away by some of our younger people, and I wanted the executive team to know it, despite how exhausted I was. One of the older members on the team was clear in his lack of desire to hear the details of the weekend. In spite of my passion for the success of the event, he still verbalized his desire to move on. Jim put his hand up, actually stopping him from finishing his sentence, and very politely, but strongly, said, "As leaders, if we ever lose our excitement for hearing about the powerful things happening in our organization, we shouldn't be on the leadership team." I was stunned. He looked at me and said, "Tell us more." That senior leader left in a huff, grumpy and angry. Jim later took me aside and gave me some of [that leader's] history and life experience to help me be more understanding and not angry or hurt with him, since I would continue to have to work with him. I was able to work with him for years without those feelings of nervousness or fear, and eventually he apologized to me, and to Jim. I learned about having someone "have your back" that day, and I also learned that forgiveness and shared relationships make leadership work.

We never know which moments in our career will be the defining moments of our leadership. Rarely do we get to pick them for ourselves. For this young woman, this meeting clearly shaped how she viewed the man who led her and how she experienced her own voice within her organization, especially in the face of her colleague's indifference and contempt. Jim also knew that to dismissively squelch the celebration and reflection of such achievement risked deflating her desire to repeat it. Yet he probably had no idea of the impact he would have on her in that meeting. It's also true, then, that we seldom get to know in which defining moments of others we may unknowingly play a part. It behooves us all, then, to be on the lookout for ways to make sure we contribute to defining moments of hope and optimism, not ones that perpetuate cynicism and discouragement.

> *Never do today that which will become someone else's*
> *responsibility tomorrow.*
> DAVID BRENT, *regional manager* WERNHAM HOGG
> *The Office*

NAVIGATING THE HAZARDS OF BEING SEEN AND HEARD

Needless to say, being seen and heard becomes more precarious when the content of what is being seen and heard is politically sensitive or difficult to discuss. Most organizations I have consulted in have their own unique portfolio of "undiscussables"—the "moose on the table," "pink elephant in the middle of the room," "naked emperor," or whatever your favorite metaphor happens to be for the gigantic issue everyone is working hard to pretend doesn't exist. To face these issues with maturity and honesty takes a level of relational courage I wish more leaders possessed.

Most of these "ignored" issues wind up getting far more attention, through the sophisticated and complex collusive mechanisms devised to mask them, than they would if they were just discussed out in the open in a productive, mature, caring conversation. These undiscussable issues range anywhere from a money-losing product that has long outlived its life cycle but is managed by a golfing buddy of the CEO's nephew, to the affair the boss is having with a manager in the department next door and the preferential treatment given to that manager, to out-and-out incompetence that gets ignored because of the silent agreements people have to protect one another in a culture filled with entitlement and mediocrity. These issues attract so much attention, they are revered. They consume endless amounts of focus and drain resources away from productive work. And to counter the reverence they are unduly accorded requires the courage of a leader's irreverence.

Organizations are littered with shot messengers. I've often fantasized about setting up a section of the executive floor with black iron gates and a sign that reads "Messenger Cemetery." For some odd reason, many leaders are more willing to tolerate the clogged-up systems and inefficient processes that become constipated with gossip, rumor, resentment, fear, and conspiracy theory, and to assassinate the courageous leaders willing to call the question on difficult problems, than to reward their courage and deal straight with the issues everyone knows stand in the way of performance. Personally, I find one of the greatest signs of respect someone in my organization can display is to come directly to me with an issue of concern, especially if that concern is *me*. For someone who reports to me to come into my office and say, "Ron, something you said in the meeting today really bothered me" tells me they trust our relationship enough to withstand that kind of feedback. As a leader, I know I am going to goof up, likely on a daily basis. Leaders are notoriously bad observers of their own reality. Regardless of how hard I try to be sensitive and aware, many of those goofs will go unnoticed by me. Those I work with could choose to conclude I am intentionally out to cause them harm. Or they could conclude I probably had no idea I'd done something to cause agitation or confusion, and then tell me so we could work it out. Nothing is more frustrating as a leader than to be in an environment in which people clearly have something on their minds, but would rather keep the leader off-balance than to just come clean.

THE POWER OF BEING SEEN AND HEARD

Listen to my colleague Ulrich's story about a high-risk situation in which a team of leaders resisted the safe route, chose not to be cowards, and stepped up to the plate to call the question at a pivotal point in their organization's life:

Alex, president of a leading loan and leasing division of a major global financial services corporation, was feeling frustrated. Six weeks into an engagement,
we had finished our diagnostic work, and one of our findings was particularly
alarming. It appeared from the verbatim data gathered in one-on-one interviews that Alex's senior team was not aligned around key elements of their
strategy—and these were core tenets, not just the details. Fundamental questions—like "What are the growth priorities?" "What capabilities need to get
developed to allow us to compete more effectively?" and "Where should the
senior team focus its energies?"—remained unanswered in the minds of key
executives. What was killing Alex was the fact that they had been at this for
eighteen months and were supposed to be well into *executing* the strategy, not
deciding *what the strategy was.* They had detailed plans for each product.
They had presented the strategy "upstairs" to Alex's bosses, and they had seemingly taken all the right steps to ensure the goals were baked into people's performance targets. Alex didn't know whether to tar and feather us as
consultants for wasting his time, haul his team in for a verbal lashing, or
both. Alex's view was that either we were wrong or the team was confused, but
he was going to get to the bottom of this. With Alex's "take no prisoners"
approach to leadership, this promised to create some more than memorable
moments for everyone involved. Frankly, I assumed it signaled the end of my
relationship with Alex.

A week later and after some deep breathing exercises, Alex met with us. After
some extensive listening to his concerns, we advised him to first engage
his team in interpreting the findings for themselves. Alex agreed to have the
team first draw their own conclusions from the data, then share his views.
We told him to let the team express any sense of violent disagreement with
any of the findings. But if they instead validated the findings, then Alex knew
something else needed to be addressed, though what that was still eluded
him. Alex was of the "hard man" school of management, and his team ranged
on a continuum from having a healthy respect for him to being deathly afraid
of him.

So as the meeting opened, here was one of those seminal moments of truth for
Alex's organization. He started the meeting gripping tightly to the big binder
with all of their strategy documents and plans. Would Alex hear what his team
really thought, or would he only hear what he probably hoped to hear—
namely, that the problem was with the data (and us as his consultants), not
with the strategy and their approach to it?

Tense though it was, it became clear early on that they thought the data was largely on target and, except for some minor points, reflective of the team's collective view. But the moose was still on the table. The moose in this situation was "we have a binder called strategy, but we aren't executing the strategy, and we don't know how." Addressing this would require not us or Alex, but one or more people on the team to name this moose; only then could the whole team and Alex productively engage the issue.

The heroic acts were small at first, with different people on Alex's team suggesting that there were some things about the strategy that might need a little more clarity. At one point, after most people had offered their initial views, Alex asked bluntly, "So you are saying in essence that even though we have done good work, we still don't really have clarity about our strategic priorities as a group?" There was a long, painful pause. Stefan, the head of strategy, then stepped up and said it best. "We have all done a lot of good work on the high concepts. The aspirations are good, but we might have skipped some steps or not taken enough time to ensure we really and truly all understood and agreed to what we were signing up for. We also didn't agree on what we would stop doing. Maybe we dove too fast into details versus making sure we had full agreement up front?"

Other people jumped in, and before Alex knew it, the group was on the track of identifying key areas where more work was needed and where there were not clear priorities. They collectively came to accept that they would have to do a lot more work around prioritizing and then managing according to those priorities rather than trying to do everything.

To say that Alex was jubilant at the end of that meeting would be a gross overstatement. But he did seem relieved. He was very disappointed that, months into a presumed rollout of the strategy, they were going to have to go back a few steps. But he also had received a huge gift from his team: the gift of telling him what they really thought. That took skill, courage, and fortitude from the team, and it took courage from Alex to be open to the possibility that maybe the problem was beyond what he'd originally thought. What he got was a level of creative engagement and ownership of the organization's future that he would never have seen had he simply pulled the team together and barked his frustration at them.

After the meeting concluded, Alex asked Stefan to join him for lunch. The two of them proceeded to have a very meaningful conversation about why the concerns hadn't surfaced before, and Stefan was able to be frank with Alex about why the team was hesitant to disagree with him, especially in meetings. Alex appeared genuinely grateful to Stefan for his honesty, and asked him to regularly come to him when he had any sense there were issues that needed to be discussed, even if they were about him. Stefan gladly said he would.

For the Moment

What were the risks Alex took in this story?

Do you have a "Stefan" around you on your team?

When was the last time you shared lunch or coffee with "Stefan"?

How would others describe your ability to deal with the "moose"?

I am routinely amazed by the desperately needed conversations among my client organizations that don't happen and the painful and costly consequences of keeping up the "all's well" veneer that will inevitably collapse under the weight of deceit anyway. It's an experience every one of us has had. And we drive home at night fantasizing about what we *wished* we had said, what we *should* have said, or what we'll say *next time* if we get the chance.

I hope you won't wait for a next time. Allow your intolerance of superficial conversation and shot messengers to crescendo into resolve. Commit to introducing deep conversation that unleashes creative thinking and accelerates momentum en route to the goals toward which you have embarked.

Language is the fundamental building block of leadership. Conversation, then, is the key to unlocking relationships in which people do their absolute best work. Without conversation and language you cannot shape direction, reframe problems, paint word pictures of desirable alternatives, and ignite passion. Conversation is the vehicle with which we live out meaningful relationships. Juanita Brown and David Isaacs have written the groundbreaking book *The World Café: Shaping Our Futures Through Conversations That Matter,* in which they express this eloquently:

> As we enter a time in which the capacity for thinking together and creating innovative solutions is viewed as critical to creating both business and social value, many of us still live with the idea that

"talk is cheap," that most people are "all talk and no action," and that we should "stop talking and get to work." Lynne Twist, a social entrepreneur who has raised millions for improving life in developing nations suggests otherwise. . . . "I believe that we don't really live in the world. We live in the conversation we have about the world . . . and over that we have absolute, omnipotent power. We have the opportunity to shape that conversation, and in so doing, to shape history."

May every conversation in which you engage be one worthy of changing history—yours, those with whom you lead, your organization's, your community's, your family's, your planet's.

> *A conversation is a dialogue, not a monologue. That's why there are so few good conversations: due to scarcity, two intelligent talkers seldom meet.*
> TRUMAN CAPOTE, *author*

THE BRIDGE TO RELATIONSHIP: ENGAGING IN DEEP CONVERSATIONS REVEALING ALL THAT CAN BE SEEN

Incumbent and emerging leaders have so much to say to one another and to learn from one another. Were you to truly "see" each other, the value of your relationships and the power of your conversations would join forces in the form of both great performance and robust community. And to engage in such conversation, here are some starter thoughts. Again, please feel free to add your own creative ideas to the list.

1. *Accept that there is no greater device than a one-on-one cup of coffee.* At the end of the day, there is no need to search out elaborate ways to engage those with whom you lead. Sitting down for a leisurely (that's a key element) cup of coffee (or tea, or sparkling water), in a setting where you can just have meaningful conversation—free of interruption, hidden agenda, and looming deadlines—will serve to enrich that conversation in ways that will undoubtedly surprise you. The time taken to enjoy a good cup of coffee will unearth perspectives, ideas, and concerns like nothing else.

2. *Set up meeting processes that foster conversation.* When it comes to how you set agendas or design meeting time, don't allow presentation time, slide decks, or highly didactic approaches to dominate. Minimize presentation, and have conversation leaders, rather than presenters, come prepared with questions to engage participants. Design meeting agendas to vary in their structure, so people are talking as a whole group, in pairs, in small groups, and so on. When people must prepare information in advance, provide simple templates on which to answer strategic questions only, and limit "show and tell" meetings by having participants read the material in advance.

3. *Confront your personal avoidance of rejection and conflict.* Start with yourself. Each of us may, to some degree, have discomfort with the idea of calling tough questions because of the possible defensiveness or conflict it may incite. Are you overly fond of being liked, needing others' approval? Do you run from any opportunity that might require you to disappoint others? If your own uneasiness is preventing you from addressing important issues with your boss, colleagues, or team, your ability to foster meaningful conversation in your organization will be limited. You must get to the bottom of your own avoidance to make sure that you can manage it in the heat of the moment. You can't recoil from circumstances requiring truth and candor.

4. *Call the question.* Someone has to go first here, so you do it. When you know there is an issue on the table being ignored, don't allow group-think or fear to sway you into silence. Don't be reckless—rehearse the messages you want to convey. Obviously there will be emotion present, otherwise it wouldn't be difficult to address. To avoid the defensiveness or discomfort that can skew the conversation, write out or prepare your nonjudgmental phrases and words in advance of the meeting. Avoid at all costs getting sucked into, or initiating, collusion before or after the meeting. Remember, if people see you colluding about someone or something else, they will naturally assume you are doing it about them with others.

5. *Pay close attention to the quiet ones.* All teams and groups have those who are less vocal than others. The verbal ones tend to use up all the air time, and those less inclined to offer their voice will either hide or be too intimidated to try and break into a conversation.

Make sure you are intentionally drawing out the thinking and views of those otherwise unlikely to volunteer them. They may not be as articulate or confident in how they express their thoughts, and the bullish players may quickly move to dismiss them if they don't get right to the point—further reinforcing their apprehension to speak. Manage those dynamics, making it clear you expect all voices to be heard, understood, and respected.

6. *Celebrate courageous conversation.* On those occasions when someone steps up and raises a difficult issue, is vulnerable with their passions and views, expresses a controversial perspective counter to the predominant views in the group, or discloses their personal uncertainty and discomfort with a decision or issue, stop the action and make sure you let others know you are grateful for such candor and honesty. Personally thank the person, especially if it is in a group setting, for trusting you and their colleagues with their ideas and feelings, and make sure there is no hint of retribution, disrespect, or dismissal. In contrast, be kind, but firmly clear with those that behave with any degree of disregard for a courageous colleague, letting your intolerance be unmistakably felt.

7. *Avoid binary problem-solving.* It's easy for conversations to deteriorate into positional debates, pitting one position against the other. At that point, it's nearly impossible for anything innovative to surface because there are only two positions being explored. That makes one person "right" and the other "wrong"—and makes proving it the mission of the debate. Make sure your problem-solving conversations are generating multiple *options* to explore rather than rival positions that must be discredited and defeated. The moment you sense "point and counterpoint" has taken over, stop the conversation and walk away. Resume later with a renewed commitment to collaboration and innovation, having abandoned the need to win.

8. *Let yourself be seen.* This doesn't mean hosting group therapy. But letting people see sides of you that you might not routinely show creates a tone of warmth and genuineness that sets others at ease and helps them drop their guard. Allowing others to see *you,* more than just your veneer, invites them to hear you more openly and to consider reciprocating. When you allow them to see you— your flaws, your passions, your convictions, your questions, your uncertainty, your pride in your work, your delight in them—you set

a context for them in which being seen is less a dangerous risk and more an opportunity to be appreciated and to grow. And when your decisions, your disappointments, and your direction must be heard, it will be within meaningful conversations in which, having been seen, your voice will be welcomed, not merely tolerated or instinctively resisted.

Remember Don and Al? I wonder how they are doing. My fear is that Don was going to soft-pedal the message, trying to make Al feel good while delivering some veiled message about how people in the room weren't getting it, and how Al needed to "slow down because, after all, they aren't as smart or experienced as you are." It'd be easy to sidestep the issue and make Al's need to adjust about the others in the room. I also had some concern that Don might inadvertently give Al a tour of history, citing "every single meeting where you present" and overwhelming Al with feelings of inadequacy on top of an already fragile ego. If I had my way (and I do, because I'm writing this), their conversation would go something along these lines:

> Don said, "Well, Al, it's funny you asked about my take on the presentation, because that's just what I wanted to talk to you about. But first, I'm curious: Why do you feel it's going as well as you do?"
>
> Al paused, clearly puzzled by Don's question. After a moment, he said, "Well, I'm seeing people nod their heads, Ed made a few comments about how exciting this was for Brookreme, and no one has really raised any concerns, so I don't really have any reason to believe otherwise. But I can tell by your comment that you don't see it that way. So what is your take?"
>
> Don's mouth got dry. He was nervous. He reached for the pitcher of water and poured himself a glass. This didn't exactly make Al feel any better. Don sat on the edge of the table, looked Al in the eye, and said very simply, "Al, I think people are overwhelmed. There is so much information we are asking them to absorb that I don't think people would know what questions to ask if they had any. But the fact that no one has asked any significant questions makes me even more worried. It's clear the data are thorough and that you've done some amazing work on this. But I think you need to remember that you've had months to live with this. Your colleagues only got these huge binders last week. And some of them have to leave next week for Asia, and if I were one of them,

I'd be terrified. Is it really reasonable to think that people this new to such complex information could absorb it at this pace without having any questions?"

Al started to interrupt, "But what could they possibly be scared of? I've given them every possible answer to—"

Don gently stuck his hand out to stop him. "Al, it's not about you. Please don't take this personally. I know how much pride you take in your work, and I believe you care a lot about us succeeding in Asia. I know you know how much is riding on this. But you need to put yourself in their shoes. You have as much as ten years' more experience than most of them. They've never launched a new business before, much less in a foreign and untested part of the world. Could you absorb hundreds of pages of minute details of information that was being presented to you? Wouldn't you feel a bit fire-hosed if you were them? Again, Al, please hear me. It's not about the quality of your work or the validity of your conclusions. It's about them—your audience. They're the ones we need to make successful. And from where I'm sitting, I don't think they'd say that's what is happening."

Al was trying not to be defensive. "How do you know? Did someone say something to you in the hallway? What did they say? If it was Sara, you know she can't stand me, and everyone knows she's as impatient as they come, so you need to take that with a grain of salt. C'mon, Don, you gotta back me on this. You know how hard I have—"

Don put his hand out again, but this time more firmly. "Al, stop! Listen to me. Look at my face. Really, listen to me, please. This is *not* about you right now. I know you take your work very personally, and that's what makes you so good. But you can't take this feedback personally. No single person said anything to me. I looked at their faces, I saw some rolling their eyes, and I saw absolute terror in others' eyes. And to be honest, Jim pulled me aside and said he had doubts about how much people were really getting this. He didn't say something to me because he doubts your ability. It's *because* of your ability that he said something, and it's because I really care about your work succeeding that I'm saying something now, while we still have some time to do some course correction. If you want your work to really make the difference for these guys that you created it to make, then we need to rethink how you help them with it. Going through page by page, number by number, scenario by scenario isn't helping them. It might feel good to you because the entire story makes sense to you. But they're hearing it for the first time. And I think there are lingering questions in their minds that a straight shot through the slides isn't going to answer for them. Can you appreciate how this could feel from their perspective?"

Al looked down and was quiet. Don didn't know if anything he'd said had gotten through or not. Al turned away and walked toward the window. It seemed to Don that he might have rubbed his eyes. Don thought to himself, *crap, I've made him cry.* But he remained silent and waited for Al to compose himself. He was very anxious about what Al was going to say, and just as anxious that the meeting was going to resume in fifteen minutes, and they hadn't even talked about what they were going to do for the rest of the day. Don felt like the agonizing silence lasted hours.

Without turning back from the window, Al finally broke the silence. At first his voice had a slight crack in it as he said, "I've given more than twenty years of my career to this company. I've always done what was asked of me, have been loyal to my bosses, and went every extra mile put in front of me. I bleed Brookreme. I've never wanted anything but for this company to turn heads in the marketplace. You know how hard it was for me when you got the job I'd waited years for because we've talked about it so many times. Hell, Don, I know I'm not as smart as you are. I get why Nancy gave you the job. And I'm happy in the job I'm in. I'm a few years away from a great retirement package, but until then, I'm gonna keep swinging for the fence while I'm here. What I don't get is why no one has ever been honest with me about how I can do my job better. Nobody's perfect. But in all my years here, you're the first person I feel who has really shot straight with me." His voice started to crack more and his bottom lip was shaking ever so slightly. "What if people had been honest with me ever since I started my career here? How much better might I have been able to become—for me, and for Brookreme—if I had been given the same quality of data about me as I've given to the organization?"

Don felt like the wind had been knocked out of him. He couldn't speak. He just waited in silence until Al finally looked up.

"Thanks. For caring enough to be honest with me."

"I'm sorry, Al. I'm so sorry that you feel it never happened before now, and I'm sorry I failed to come to you sooner. It's clear we have a lot more to talk about on this—we're far from done. And I mean that."

Al moved to the front of the room toward his binders. "Don't worry. I'll make sure we're not done. I have a lot of questions after today. But right now, it would appear we have a meeting to redesign. So how would you suggest we proceed?"

Over the next twenty minutes or so, while people were trickling in from the break, Al and Don worked on a very creative approach to the meeting that would allow people to safely surface concerns, anxieties, and ideas for executing the strategy. They never went back to the slides. They also agreed to host three or four intensive sessions over the coming weeks for folks to come and get personal coaching, problem solving, and consultation from Don's entire department until they felt confident they understood and could execute the plan.

The next day, Al and Don went to lunch together. The lunch lasted nearly three hours, during which they finished at least one pot of coffee.

For the Moments Yet to Come . . .

1. When was the last time you engaged in a meaningful conversation that surfaced important insights?

2. What causes you to put on your veneer? In what types of situations are you most likely to "hide" and withhold your real views?

3. How do you feel when you are in a conversation in which you know others aren't being forthright with their views? Have you ever asked if you've done something to make them uncomfortable by being candid?

4. What ideas have you seen wasted because they never got the chance to be heard by others? What breakthroughs have you seen as a result of someone taking the risk to offer radical ideas?

5. How encouraging of meaningful conversation would you say your organization is?

CHAPTER THREE

A VOICE AT THE TABLE

The Death of Deception, The Dare of Invitation

All deception in the course of life
Is indeed nothing else but a lie reduced to practice,
And falsehood passing from words into things.

Robert Southey

Opportunity: Extend genuine invitations and dispense with faux involvement to maximize passion and commitment.

Everyone dreads situations like this:

> Nancy knew the conversation with the Sydney team was going to be tough. Though they had spent years building strategies to break into the Pacific Rim market, none of their suggestions had succeeded. Nancy asked Jim to refrain from disclosing the activity under way at Brookreme headquarters to launch the new Pacific Rim venture until she'd personally had the chance to meet with the Sydney team.
>
> Brookreme's Australia division was led by Elliot, who had been in charge down under for nearly five years. He was a native New Zealander and another of Brookreme's rising stars. Nancy had believed Elliot's "hometown boy" characteristics made him the perfect choice to capture the Australian market. She had been right—Elliot had done a fabulous job. Revenues in Australia had almost doubled during his tenure, and Elliot had established important bridgeheads for Brookreme in Malaysia and Seoul. He was passionate about making his mark, and he assumed that his track record made a promotion from division president of Australia to regional president of the Pacific Rim nearly certain. Though a lot of people were aware of Elliot's ambition in this sphere, no one was offended. Elliot was committed and talented, and although he had a visibly strong ego, he was not at all obnoxious or condescending. He had built a team of young, go-getter types who were quite loyal to him and

eager to share in his success. Elliot's team supported his ambition and looked forward to a widening sphere of influence and opportunity for themselves when Elliot moved up.

Nancy's challenge was to burst this bubble for Elliot and his team without losing them altogether as high performers in Australia. She knew that a teleconference would do more harm than good. She had to break this news in person.

Despite Jim's best attempts to position Nancy's visit with Elliot and his team, Elliot misinterpreted the purpose of the trip. He thought her "I want to talk about what's happening in Asia," meant that this was his opportunity to sell his team's comprehensive, robust strategy for taking Asia by storm to the CEO in person. Elliot felt he had done enough homework to understand why they hadn't been successful previously, and he believed he could convince Nancy to fund what he considered to be a surefire strategy.

Nancy arrived in Sydney and went straight to her hotel room. She discovered a huge gift basket of local treats waiting for her, as well as a variety of gifts and beautiful photograph books from China and Malaysia. There was a handwritten note: "Great to have you here with us, Nancy. I'm looking forward to an exciting conversation about our future in Asia. Rest well. Best, Elliot."

Nancy could feel the tension building in her temples. She knew this could get ugly if Elliot felt completely cut out of Brookreme's push into Asia. She needed him to take ownership of helping make it successful, but she also needed him to take ownership of the fact that, despite years of funding and effort, he had not succeeded. She simply had to push forward with an alternative approach. It would require a delicate balance of support and clarity to keep Elliot's ego intact. She knew that if he got angry and resigned, it could cause a ripple effect and an exodus of Elliot's entire devoted team, each handpicked by him. Her anxiety and jet lag conspired to guarantee a sleepless night.

When Nancy arrived at Brookreme's Australian offices in downtown Sydney, she was greeted warmly by the receptionist, and she took note of her welcome on the lobby marquee. Elliot's assistant, Ethel, came down to escort her up to Elliot's office, offering her coffee on the way. Nancy gladly accepted that offer, privately wishing it could include a shot of something stronger. Elliot bounded out of his office in his usual bigger-than-life style and greeted Nancy with a warm hug. She genuinely liked him and, despite what was about to unfold, enjoyed having him as a colleague. They spent about half an hour catching up while walking around the offices and saying hello to the staff.

When they walked into the conference room adjacent to Elliot's office, Nancy was taken aback to see Elliot's team all gathered around the table with the projector on and a presentation entitled "Brookreme Takes Asia by Storm" ready to go. There were various Asia-Pacific artifacts creatively displayed around the room and glowing smiles on the faces of the entire team. Nancy smiled warmly back at them, but her stomach was one big knot. She'd had to put on her game face before, but this was a whole new level of acting for her— entirely out of her experience. She thought, *If I can make it through this, I'll win an Academy Award for sure.*

The presentation opened like a Broadway production, with music, film, photos, and art combining in a high-tech multimedia experience that transported everyone into a virtual-reality Brookreme Asia-Pacific experience. Each person around the table presented a piece after an animated opening by Elliot. With image after image, Nancy's anxiety level rose as she saw exactly why Elliot's team had been so far off the mark in previous years. Their assumptions about the market's maturity and readiness for Brookreme's products were flawed. They had not done the necessary research to understand the nuances of how to connect with an emerging market, and were treating each Asia-Pacific opportunity with a one-size-fits-all entry strategy—very similar to the ones that had made them so successful in Australia. Nancy now saw the extent to which Elliot's past successes were causing him to miss the challenges ahead. She regretted that this insight had not come to her sooner.

Nancy also knew that with each passing segment of the presentation, her questions and even her attentive silence were being misinterpreted as support. She realized that from the moment Jim had made the call to Elliot over a month ago, she had unwittingly led Elliot and his team to believe that they would be at the center of Brookreme's Asia-Pacific play—and that was the exact opposite of what had to happen. Yes, they had an important role to play, but not the one they'd come to believe so passionately that they would. And on each face in the room, Nancy could see the conviction that the team had already sealed the deal. Nancy knew that pulling the rug out from under them now would be an unmitigated disaster.

At the end of the nearly two-hour presentation, there were the obligatory high fives and congratulatory exchanges. Although Nancy was very measured in her words to them (with noncommittal comments like "It's clear you guys have done a lot of work," and "Your energy and passion are infectious"), she knew this was going to be one of the most difficult conversations of her career as

CEO. In essence, how was she going to take one of her star employees—whom she respected and planned on grooming for bigger things—and cut him off at the knees? All she could think to herself was, *Being the leader sucks.*

For their part, the team members were beside themselves with anticipation of Nancy's endorsement. All she had to do was say the word and they'd be off like gangbusters. Nancy did what any good leader would do—she punted.

"Guys, I know you want me to give you the green flag right now, but please understand that you've given me a *lot* to consider. I could easily give in to the temptation to be carried away by your passion, but that would be irrespon-sible of me. There are lots of considerations we have to make, and we need to get these ideas in front of key players back in Chicago. Please don't hear that as a lack of genuine appreciation for your work, or some withdrawal of sup-port. If Brookreme is going to be successful in Asia, we've all got to be very calculated every step of the way. I'm sure you guys, more than anyone else, can understand that, since you've taken a run at this several times. I don't mean that as a dig, so please don't take it that way. I know how frustrated you have been, and how hard you have worked to get us off the ground in Asia. And I know you want *this* time to work, and no one wants success more than I do. The board and the analysts are watching closely, so let's work together to show them we can do this. Be patient with me while I give this the kind of thought it deserves."

As she walked out of the conference room, she could see a variety of reactions on their faces. Some heard the genuineness of her remarks. Others clearly felt screwed. She thought to herself, *Well, at least I didn't lie to them. Technically.*

After she left, the team launched into a feverish attempt to decode Nancy's words. The gamut of reactions was wide. Everything from, "Cool—she's going back to get us the funding," all the way to, "She has no intention of support-ing us and she didn't have the heart, or the guts, to come clean with us."

Elliot was too proud to push for more details. He also knew she had phone meetings to be on, and then they had to leave for several customer visits Elliot had arranged. She was also going to appear as a guest on a local business radio show that evening. He had packed her entire visit with meetings with key employees, suppliers, and customers, as well as some fun visits to the local sights and, of course, some great restaurants.

Nancy had several more sleepless nights, and after the first couple she couldn't blame her jet lag. She felt she had led people to believe something that wasn't true. She certainly had not meant to, but that didn't matter now. She'd walked the empowerment tightrope before—a constant razor's-edge balance of how much rein to give and how much to pull in. She'd been in plenty of meetings where she'd had to gently guide people to decisions she knew had to be made while allowing them to think it was their idea, and she'd also been in meetings where her own wrong-minded ideas were scrapped. At times she felt genuine, and at times she felt deviously manipulative. Not surprisingly, there were times she was seen as both. She feared she would be seen in the absolutely worst light by the end of this trip. How could she possibly reconcile the path she knew to be right with finding a way to let Elliot and his team down?

For the Moment

How often does your role require "Academy Award–winning" performances?

How might you define your own "empowerment tightrope"?

Knowing that Nancy has to break some tough news, how would you counsel her to use the rest of her time in Australia?

Nancy's gotten herself into quite the dilemma. At this point, it really doesn't matter what she could or should have done differently—last month or last year—to avoid this hazardous intersection with Elliot. Inadvertently, she's laid the groundwork for a disaster and now she has to deal with it. What would you do if you found yourself in her shoes?

POWER AND INCLUSION: COLLIDING FORCES

For many years, the success of one's climb up the corporate ladder was defined by having a seat at the table. Many became disillusioned by learning that a *seat* was actually all it was—observer status without a voice. The sanctions on opening one's mouth, especially to express a view contrary to the predominant view at the table (most often that of the boss), were career-killing.

Every time I speak at conferences or to client groups about this aspect of leadership, I ask, "How many of you, by a show of hands, have been in meetings where you knew you were being schmoozed into thinking you were involved in the formation of a decision or direction that in fact had already been decided before the conversation began?" In all the times I've asked the question, I've never seen fewer than 80 to 90 percent of the people in the room raise their hands. And many raise them with a zealous force and disgruntled moans that suggests it's a routine experience.

It certainly wasn't supposed to be this way. Over the course of the past thirty years, hundreds of articles and books have been written about workplace empowerment—engaging employees in the service of building greater ownership and commitment. A spate of books—like *The Empowered Manager, Teaching Elephants to Dance*, and *Zapp! The Lightning of Empowerment*—promised a panacea for employees who felt powerless to control their own destinies, stifled by bureaucracies, and sapped of creative energy. The idea was to get away from situations in which people were allegedly responsible but the boss actually made the decisions. As people grappled with this idea, however, it became apparent that there were some resistant ideological barriers to empowerment built into the power structure of most organizations. Thomas Potterfield's book *The Business of Employee Empowerment: Democracy and Ideology in the Workplace* and *One Minute Manager* author Ken Blanchard's book *Empowerment Takes More Than a Minute* looked at breaking through these barriers through information sharing, redrawing boundaries, and replacing hierarchy with teams.

However, the persistent problem since the seventies has been one of degree. Too little empowerment feels fake—people feel they are going through the motions, but at the end of the day the boss still calls the shots, and everybody knows it. Too much empowerment, on the other hand, leads to mayhem. Decision making becomes too decentralized and teams have a weakened sense of accountability to the core mission. In this situation, team morale can go up but business results can go down. It is difficult to find the right balance. And given the dangers of too much empowerment and the natural inclination today's leaders have to refrain from letting go, many err on the side of paying lip service to empowerment while retaining full control.

There's no "I" in "team." But then there's no "I" in
"useless smug colleague" either. And there's four in
"platitude-quoting idiot." Go figure.
             David Brent, *regional manager* Wernham Hogg
                               The Office

From Theory to Deception:
The Glamour of Faux Inclusion

Leaders get the concept behind empowerment. Command-and-control leadership disenfranchises employees, and they resent being merely robotic pawns in someone else's game. But many leaders have never come to terms with what empowerment really means to their sense of control. Most leaders who got caught on the wave of "make them feel included" genuinely believed it was important for people to have a sense of real ownership. The problem is, they came to believe they could *bestow* that sense of ownership, failing to realize that people had to *choose* ownership. Does this belief arise because incumbent leaders are on some Machiavellian mission to manipulate everyone they lead? Of course not. I believe many of them genuinely do want to hear what others have to say, so that others feel included in the decisions that affect them and have a personal stake in the organization's destiny. But the DNA of "my way or the highway" is so embedded that the concept of suspending one's biases long enough to risk being converted to someone else's point of view, is a painful concept for many leaders.

For emerging leaders, the jig is up for faux inclusion. Sadly, most go into meetings now *expecting* a ruse from incumbent leaders. They know the drill: a brainstorming session in which flip charts and whiteboards get filled with ideas, detailed surveys get completed about what people think of this or that, focus groups are conducted to "get to the bottom of employees' concerns," and consultants are hired to interview key opinion leaders to find out what they think about a given strategy. And then, as if by some magical, serendipitous coincidence, the data supports the conclusions and direction the boss originally advocated in the first place. Of course, selected *words and phrases* from the process are retrofitted into the decision as evidence that "we all had a say in it." But everyone knows exactly what happened, and no one believes for a minute the decision wasn't made long before anyone was ever asked what they thought.

Lately, emerging leaders are broadcasting their intolerance of such manipulation. Even if the leader truly was suspending disbelief and genuinely wanted to hear others' views, many emerging leaders are cutting to the quick at the outset and saying things like, "Look, please don't waste my time. If you don't really want to know what I think, and all you want to hear is that I agree with you, can we just skip to that and forget the charade of my having to make it look like I came to the same conclusion as you?" One senior executive told me of his utter astonishment when one of his team members basically came right out and said this to him.

Emerging leaders risk cutting themselves off from being genuinely influential by withholding their voices in a premature protest of a deception that may not exist. Again, many incumbent leaders actually *do* want to know what others think and are willing to act upon what they learn. But if emerging leaders conclude that their voice is just being exploited by anyone who appears to be asking them for input, they will miss the very opportunity for influence that they claim is often withheld from them. Emerging leaders would do well to instead courageously extend their voice in the hope of making a difference. Rather than giving in to cynicism that tempts them to be silent, emerging leaders need to rise to the occasion with hope and offer their voice.

> *Being powerful is like being a lady [or a gentleman]. If*
> *you have to tell people you are, you aren't.*
> MARGARET THATCHER, *British prime minister,*
> *1979–1990*

THE MYTH OF EMPOWERMENT: BORROWED POWER

The fundamental misconception of empowerment—giving power away to others—is that power was never yours to give in the first place. Power that can be exercised only with another's permission isn't legitimate power. It's just *borrowed.* And anything borrowed eventually must be returned. Everyone resents the use of *borrowed* power, especially emerging leaders. The exercise of borrowed power usually begins with someone else's name—usually the one with the *real* power. "I was just talking with Bill this morning and he said he just found out yesterday that . . .," Or "Well, Jeff asked me to find out about . . ." Or "I didn't get the impression from Anne that's what she wanted. She told me after the meeting that . . . ," or "I can just ask Ed tonight when I see him for dinner at his house . . . oh, you weren't invited too?" It's irritating and cowardly. But it does induce fear in many, especially fellow incumbent leaders for whom power is a volatile topic. To many, power is a zero-sum game: the more of it someone else has, the less they have. By contrast, most emerging leaders couldn't care less whose name you drop or what you think you know. If they don't agree, they're not playing.

One's power is really one's capacity to *influence,* not the degree to which one can dominate. And it certainly isn't the degree to which one can leverage the power of someone else. The exercise of power, regardless of its source, is the choice of the person exercising it, and to respond to power is the choice of the person at whom the influence is being directed. Power, then, is never absolute. It exists only in *relationship.* One can't exercise power if someone else isn't going to *respond.*

According to theorists John French and Bertram Raven, there are six sources of power from which one can influence:

- Positional—based on a person's role, which gives them the ability to give orders and make demands
- Referent—based on being liked or admired
- Coercive—based on having the ability to control something someone else needs
- Reward—based on the ability to grant or distribute rewards, including money, recognition, promotions, referrals, or other favors
- Expertise—based on having knowledge and skills that others do not possess or that are needed for a specific task
- Experience—based on having information or perspective that others do not have

Effective leaders employ multiple sources of influence according to the circumstances at hand. They realize it isn't just their own voice that ultimately determines how power is exercised, it's also the voices of those whom they are trying to influence. Power isn't power until someone acts. And if the only response to exerted power is *compliance,* the power is going to be short-lived, and eventually will exhaust the leader, who must continually exert increasing degrees of that power just to get anything done.

Listen to my colleague Mindy's story of her client, and the power of what happens when someone extends a genuine invitation to have a voice at the table:

> A government-owned utility company went through a twelve-month period of extreme disruption and negative events, including accusations of inappropriate spending of company funds by its leaders and large-scale downsizing to cover cash shortfalls. These events eventually led to the dismissal of the CEO and the forced retirement of many of the senior leadership. A board member was asked to act as interim CEO until a new leader was named. After a period of five months, an internal candidate was selected as CEO. The candidate had been the president of the largest business unit and acting COO. He had been hired a year previously from a large utility company in another country and was not closely associated with the former CEO or leadership team. He had remained an "outsider" because of his short tenure, his lack of association with politics, and his style, which many found to be starkly forthcoming and decisive.
>
> One of the critical priorities in his new role was to create a structure that provided the right level of operational oversight without rebuilding a bureaucracy that had led to cost inefficiencies and mismanagement. His strengths as a leader were operational in nature, including an ability to understand and direct business decisions at every level, a focused delivery of results, and connection to all employees. But in his new role he was forced to spend time with external stakeholders including a new board, a set of government constituents, and a media focus that surpassed anything he had dealt with previously. Because of this, he was convinced the appropriate structure would include a COO who reported directly to him. As we began to discuss the options and planned for change, it was obvious he felt he had the right answer and that other choices were not to be considered. But because of the newness of his board relationship, he felt unable to create a position of that scope and compensation without their full support.
>
> His feeling that he had reached a stalemate with his board created an opening for me to present different points of view. We had several conversations about a

"continuum of alternatives for operational governance." Some were far outside his box of thinking. Opening this window into what felt like unrealistic alternatives did cause him to at least consider some new perspectives. We then built a process that included talking to the top eight leaders in the organization—many of whom would report to a COO if one was appointed. The CEO agreed to engage them in a conversation around their ideas to drive operational governance. After a series of confidential one-on-one interviews, we had three distinct options that were well thought out and fit the organization. Each had a set of costs and benefits identified, along with critical success factors for making them work. This report set the context for a session between the CEO and his direct reports.

In this session, the CEO began by admitting his own bias for appointing a COO and stating that were it not for the restrictions of the board he might have already gone down that path. He spoke strongly about his operational needs, and he steered far from the three alternatives being presented. It was clear the team was starting to become discouraged, as though presenting their recommendations was really futile. He was already determined to appoint a COO regardless of how the day went, so team members felt he should just get on with it and skip the charade.

The session was designed so that each alternative (one of which was to have a COO) had assigned advocates who presented its supporting details. After about four hours, the session felt like a merry-go-round. It was clear the CEO was feeling directly accountable to the board for operational results but knew he could no longer work to ensure these himself. Although he could see the need to leverage his team, he just hadn't come to trust them yet. Politically, it wasn't apparent to him which were supporters and which were just previous regime leftovers. He bluntly shared these concerns with his team in the room. Not exactly a moment of rallying the troops.

In response, they shared some of their own trepidations about his leadership and the changes he was putting in place. They acknowledged his needs for operational control and even admitted their difficulty in trusting him. They proposed an entirely different way to get to the operational results he required, an alternative not at all considered among the three presented that day.

It was clear the CEO was very uncomfortable. It was also clear he just wanted his way. But having gotten this far into the conversation, he knew that if he just put in a COO, the risks of his team's checking out—or, worse, sabotaging him—were high. He ended up slightly modifying their recommendations. By the end of the session he felt comfortable enough with their commitment to his operational goals that he presented a plan to the board that included an operations council, led by rotating leadership of the team. As CEO, he felt he now had a group of leaders invested in him and the success of the organization. He also knew the key players and didn't worry about getting filtered information as he might have through a COO. As direct reports to the CEO, they felt like they had influenced his thinking—something that had never happened before. They also felt they were able to step up to leadership roles they believed they could handle. The board was comfortable with the CEO's decisions because it allowed them to emphasize fiscal responsibility and gave them insight into the succession plan for the future.

Had the CEO's team not had their voices at the table, it's highly unlikely the team would ever have felt vested in the operational turnaround of the organization. And worse, a COO would have been set up to fail.

For the Moment

Of French and Raven's "six bases of social power," where are you strongest? Weakest?

Are you hopeful or skeptical about Mindy's story? Why?

Can you risk removing the "filters" in your organization? How?

Many Voices at the Table: Noodle Teams

One of the most insatiably curious leaders I have ever had the privilege of working alongside is Mike Roberts. I've had a front-row seat for the story of Mike's career at McDonald's, watching him move through the organization from a division president in the western U.S. to president of the McDonald's U.S. operation, to his current position as president of McDonald's Corporation worldwide. Because I'll tell him when I think he's made a mistake, or remind him about one of his blind spots, I feel no hesitation in saying he is one of the most talented and generous executives I've ever had the honor of working with.

About seven years ago, he instituted a process called "Noodle Teams." A Noodle Team is a handpicked set of people from both inside and outside the corporation who meet four times in a given year for three days at a time. Employees from around the region or world, suppliers, owner operators, and external experts gather, and basically it's "gloves off." They put the toughest challenges on the table to be innovatively dealt with. Not only are folks expected to tell the emperor he has no clothes, but they are expected to figure out what kind of clothes the emperor needs. They get to deal straight with the most painful issues the corporation is facing in a safe environment where they have no fear of retaliation, judgment, or political retribution. They aren't just invited to think about issues—they are expected to help resolve them. They don't just come and dump the issues on Mike's desk, either. They take ownership of them and commit to addressing them.

Here's how Mike describes his reasoning for Noodle Teams:

> This is essentially my window into the entire company. If something is brought up here, I know it's important. I get to see the organization in a different light, and govern differently as a result. I store the issues I hear sometimes, and at the appropriate moment, I am prepared with perspectives and ideas to ask relevant questions. I get to hear from people I would otherwise never get to interact with, and because most of them have spoken to ten or fifteen other people prior to coming, I really get the benefit of broad views that would never surface if I only talked to people in the C-suite. When you work in a franchised environment, the ability to listen, *really LISTEN*, is critical to relationships. I suspend my natural reactions to defend myself against some of the really harsh, and even sometimes unfounded feedback, and ask myself, "Why is this person seeing it this way?" I really want to understand. In that way, not only do they feel heard, but I get critical insights and learning you just can't put a price on.

> One executive recently commented to me at the end of a Noodle Team meeting, "I don't know how you sit there and just take it without getting defensive. Every role model I've seen would have stopped the conversation cold and launched into lengthy explanations, justifications, and ultimately, dismissal of the points being raised. But it's pretty clear—you actually want to hear what people have to say."

The work that has come out of the Noodle Teams has been incredible. It's not easy to get anything done in a corporation of 1.4 million employees and 29,000 restaurants. If I can't be sure I've heard from as many of them as possible, and they from me, and that as many of them as are able are owning the decisions and actions in their regions and departments, we'd be in trouble.

Jason Greenspan, a member of Mike's team, has this to say about the Noodle Teams:

> The Noodle Team is a powerful way for Mike to hear what's really happening deep within the organization . . . the stuff that's usually filtered long before it gets to his level. And this feedback is quite candid—what he's doing that's not working, what people are saying in the hallways, where the organization needs to intensify his focus, where the focus isn't having the intended impact, and where and how his messages are resonating with different audiences. During all of this, Mike listens. He takes notes. He probes. He asks questions. He seeks clarification. But he never pushes back. He never gets defensive. He never asks for sources. He trusts the team. He trusts their perspective. He trusts that the information they're bringing him is accurate and representative of what's happening in the organization. They've told him where and how and why business is softening . . . in an "early warning system" kind of way. Following the meeting, Mike and others will review all of the notes, prioritize what we heard, and then immediately incorporate the key items into his ongoing leadership plan—be it decisions he needs to make, how and where he spends his time, modifications to his leadership impact, or dozens of other recommendations/actions.
>
> Each meeting provides enough fodder for a year's worth of work. We've made major changes in how we've organized the corporation, how we spend and focus our media dollars, and how HR supports the field as a result of ideas and conversations that came from Noodle Teams.

The Risk of Invitation: Setting Boundaries and Letting Go

So what prevents leaders from relinquishing the charade of making it appear as though others are included and daring to extend the invitation to have a legitimate voice at the table? Many leaders have told me they are secretly plagued by the following underlying questions as they face moments that offer opportunities to let go. (This section could well be titled "Confessions of a Control Freak.") It's not an exhaustive, clinically researched list, so feel free to add your own neuroses and phobias to it.

1. *What if I lose control?* Many leaders, especially incumbent leaders, operate with an underlying assumption they must be "in control." Of course, there is partial truth here. It is a leader's responsibility to ensure that her organization is performing as well as it can, being fiscally responsible, operating with integrity, keeping commitments to those it serves, and treating those in the organization respectfully. What becomes difficult for many leaders is to trust that others in the organization are often better equipped to see to these standards than they are. It is a leader's role to set clear expectations and then allow others to have control over meeting those expectations. Relinquishing control is the only way to ensure having any.

2. *What if I am wrong?* Leaders hate to be wrong. It's odd, because the irony is that often they *are* wrong, and they know it. It's a miracle that leaders are ever right, given that they have access to the least complete set of reliable data. Starting with the assumption "I don't know" instead of "I already know" is a far better way of getting to the best answers and solutions, forsaking the false notion that there are ever completely "right" answers.

3. *What if they take advantage of the freedom I give them?* The plain truth is, some will. But most won't. Some leaders aren't ready for the responsibility that comes with having authority. They lack the maturity or experience necessary to be judicious, thoughtful, and caring in how they exercise their influence. But it is a leader's job to assess that and to offer a measure of inclusion commensurate with a person's readiness to participate. My advice to my clients is to err on the side of giving more, not less. Yes, when some take advantage of you, it will hurt. You might even feel betrayed. But that consequence pales in comparison to withholding true invitation and stifling the voices of those genuinely ready to participate and contribute in profound ways.

4. *What if I look incompetent or indecisive to others?* Relax. In some situations, you already do. Get over it. Contrary to false assump-

tions, most people in organizations aren't holding up the yardstick of "How many decisions did my leader make this week?" to assess how effective they think you are. True, being indecisive is a painful reality for many leaders, and the resulting obstruction to performance can be agonizing and paralyzing to an organization. But most leaders lacking a needed bias for action will eventually derail. Overcompensating—for fear of being seen that way—by making *all* of the decisions won't get you seen as more competent or decisive; you'll just look like a very accomplished micromanager.

5. *What if someone else has a better idea or, worse, a brilliant idea that upstages me?* Accept it, and celebrate it—that's what you should want. The hardest thing to let go of for leaders who have grown up in an organization and been rewarded for their brilliance is the gratification that comes from being seen as brilliant. Not having the most brilliant idea doesn't make you any less brilliant. But as a leader, your job isn't to be brilliant. Your job is to facilitate the brilliance *of others*. If you always have to be the smartest kid in the class, you will systematically dismantle your greatest weapon—the ideas and passion of those you lead.

6. *What if I relinquish power and they have a terrible idea that fails?* You can't prevent others from failing. We all know our greatest lessons in life came from how we navigated failure. Yet as leaders (and often as parents) letting those in our charge fail is a grueling experience. We'd rather rush in and rescue them. In so doing, we love them into incompetence. Sometimes you will relinquish decision making to others, they will ignore the input you offered, and then they will astound you with far better outcomes than you could have imagined. And sometimes you will relinquish decision making and they will ignore the input you offered, do their own thing, and fail. There's no shortcut through that, and attempting to avert or delay it will only force you into the role of buck-stopper on every decision.

THE POWER OF INVITATION: UNCOVERING REAL POWER

The art of invitation is the constant balance of blending your voice with the voices of others. Sometimes you get to be lead singer, and sometimes you get to sing backup. Sometimes you just have to be one of the choir. Regardless of which, you must learn to enjoy all these roles. As one CEO told me quite bluntly regarding leaders who can't let go, "If you think you can do it all yourself, that's fine. Go ahead and try. But I don't want to own your stock."

To be clear, there is a significant distinction between relinquishing control and abandoning others. Many leaders find it difficult to navigate the all-or-nothing dangerously binary view of this. As a leader, your question is not, "Do I decide, or do they decide?" The question is, "What degree of my involvement will be needed for the optimal decision?" One of my favorite questions to ask people in my organization is, "What do you need from me?" Not surprisingly, they tell me. Sometimes the answer is, "Nothing." Sometimes it's, "I'll get on your calendar—I need some help with a specific part of this." Sometimes it's, "I need you to run interference." And sometimes it's, "Can you brainstorm with me?" It frees me up immensely from having to feel like I must navigate all of the decision making alone. It also creates a sense of deep ownership and commitment from leaders who know they will be accountable for the results to which they commit. Again, very liberating for me.

For incumbent leaders, one painful challenge comes from the inherent resistance many emerging leaders have to *any* involvement from their leaders. They are so conditioned to expect the abuse of power that sometimes even the slightest hint of input or advice from incumbents is seen as overcontrolling or criticizing. I've heard incumbent leaders lament their frustrations over emerging leaders' expectations of total autonomy. And often the sad result is that incumbent leaders respond to their frustrations by simply taking complete control, exhausted from the debate. In the end, they wind up proving emerging leaders right—control is all they ever wanted. A sad, repeating cycle.

Emerging leaders, by contrast, have an exceptional desire to include others and reach consensus. They appear quite committed to never being seen as power-hungry or overcontrolling. And I applaud them for this! My concern, however, is how these leaders will navigate the treacherous waters of a deadlock. If you condition those you lead with the notion that every decision will be reached by consensus, when you come upon the inevitable decision that requires someone to "make the call" you will wind up causing the very disappointment, even anger, you worked so hard to avoid. You will need to strike a balance early in your relationships so people understand how you intend to participate in decisions with them. We heard time and again about leaders who set aside their own agendas to listen, question, brainstorm, and create with those they were leading. Even when interactions were painful, emerging leaders appreciate the value of being included. Emerging leaders want to know that those who lead them are "fair, direct, challenging, supportive, and clearly in charge." The words that emerging leaders repeatedly used hold clear contradictions—the true reality of relational leadership. Being supportive but clearly in charge requires an artful degree of balance not easily struck.

There is simply no substitute for the awe-inspiring beauty that comes from leaders *extending invitations to leaders* and leaders *accepting invitations to lead.* If you hope to see unbridled passion and unwavering commitment from those with whom you lead, there is no way to that end but through the unleashing of their voices and the careful blending in of your own.

> *Only passions, great passions, can elevate the soul to great things.*
>
> Denis Diderot
> *Pensées Philosophiques*

The Bridge to Relationship: Renouncing Faux Inclusion and Extending Invitations That Unleash Passion

The voices of incumbent and emerging leaders need not be discordant or dissonant to one another. Blended well, the force to be released from their combined voice can enable them to accomplish great things born out of great passions and unleash a formidable competitive threat to others in the market. Here are some thoughts on harmonizing those voices. By all means, broaden the list with your own successes.

1. *Set clear decision-making parameters.* Never leave this to interpretation. Let people know what involvement you intend to have

in any given decision. When you clarify the degree of involvement you intend to have in a particular decision, be equally clear about why you will be involved to that degree. For example, decisions of strategic importance may require a different form of your voice than decisions during an immediate crisis. Without knowing your rationale, it's entirely too easy for people to make unfounded assumptions about the degree to which you are involved in a decision. Invite people to ask questions once you've disclosed your thinking.

2. *Don't withdraw or pout when you have to "sing backup."* Regardless of where you sit, there will be decisions, projects, issues, for which your voice will not be substantially needed. This includes when you are the boss. When others' voices prevail, "outsing," or require yours to be softened, don't give into the natural but petty temptation to withdraw your support. We all struggle with not getting our way sometimes. Show those with whom you lead that you can be big about it. Overtly offer support to others whose voice(s) found their way to center stage, and sing backup with all your humble might.

3. *Put your biases on the table.* When you are struggling with relinquishing control, admit it, and invite others into the struggle. Whether it is being wed to a particular conclusion, being personally connected to a project or desired outcome, or your lack of faith in others to achieve the results you want, let people know you are struggling. If you participate in silence, or keep drawing attention back to the idea you hope is selected, the dynamic will quickly turn to one of "who can outmanipulate whom." Tell people why you have particular interest or conviction about certain outcomes or approaches, and invite people to *test* those assumptions.

4. *Know your tendencies for control.* Most of us don't naturally acknowledge our own shortfalls when it comes to control. Some of us like it too much, some of us don't like it enough. Certain circumstances will push our buttons, causing us to seize all the control available or run as far as we can from having to take control. It's important that you know which you do when. Pay attention to the emotional reactions you have when situations develop outside your expectations. When circumstances deviate from your expectations, do you allow yourself to be pleasantly surprised? Do

you freeze in frustration? Do you demand explanations from others? Do you flee? Knowing your own impulses will help you guide them when navigating through the muddy waters of complex decision making.

5. *When invited to the table, show up.* Nothing discourages leaders more than when they extend a genuine invitation that gets rejected. Sometimes the invitations we receive won't come in the form of the precise dream opportunity we imagined. One CEO told me that when he offered broader assignments to promising leaders, sometimes they would respond with, "Well, for the right opportunity, I'd be willing to move." He knew that was code for, "Make me a CEO and don't make it hard." Sometimes life just doesn't serve up opportunities that match our wish lists. When leaders offer opportunities to have a voice at the table, even if it's not the voice we'd hoped they'd offer, or even if it might require more of us than we want—or have confidence—to give, put your skin in the game and give it your best effort.

6. *Delight in one another's voices.* Nothing is more cacophonous than the voices of leaders in competition with one another. The one-upmanship that takes place in distrusting environments where people feel pitted against one another for the next promotion or accolade can be toxic. When someone you lead with engages passionately in their work, whether as a lead voice or a supporting voice, enjoy it. Whether it's your boss, peer, or direct report, learn to welcome and take pleasure in the contributions of others.

7. *Never pretend you want input you really don't.* It is never an act of "professional courtesy" to ask others for input that you actually don't want or have no intention of using. You can rationalize doing it all you like—*I wanted them to feel good, I wanted to cover my bases and make sure I wasn't missing anything, I didn't want others thinking I didn't care about their views,* and on and on. The bottom line is, if you aren't willing to be genuinely influenced to some degree, even to have your mind completely changed, by the voices of others, don't ask for them. Deal with the consequences of that, but don't try to have your cake and eat it too—all the control you want with everyone around you feeling passionate, engaged, and committed. It'll never work. Trust me. If this were as obvious as it sounds, organizational life, and performance, would look a lot different than it does.

When last we left our heroes at Brookreme, Nancy was headed in to have a very unpleasant conversation with Elliot. She now has a set of key leaders who believe their voices have been invited and heard, and she realizes she was complicit in leading them on. So many leaders find themselves needlessly at the messy crossroads of having made a mistake and feeling forced to make more mistakes or cover up the initial mistake, all in the deluded hope of not disenfranchising others. We know it's a hallucinatory effort, but we try anyway. My hope for Nancy is that she can at least make her desires known to Elliot and avoid making things worse by perpetuating his already-distorted beliefs about what his role will be in taking Brookreme to Asia. Let's see how she does.

> When the car pulled up in front of Brookreme's offices, Nancy let the driver know how long she'd be and asked to just leave her luggage in the car. Elliot greeted Nancy at his office door, and Ethel offered Nancy coffee. "Cream, no sugar, right?" she asked cheerfully. Nancy nodded gratefully.
>
> Elliot and she made small talk about the great visits they'd had over the last few days and the exquisite meal they'd enjoyed the night before, and they laughed recalling the odd sense of humor of one of their customers. Ethel quietly set the coffee on the table near the sitting area and left, shutting the door behind her. Elliot and Nancy went over to the sofa and sat across from each other. The awkwardness was tangible, and both their tension levels were visible. Elliot had tried not to wonder too much why it seemed Nancy had been elusive over the last couple of days, not taking any of his hints to revisit the Asia discussion. Nancy knew Elliot was curious, but appreciated his show of restraint not to push her for more information, especially since they'd really not had any extended time together alone. She broke the ice.
>
> "Look, Elliot, I know you probably want more reaction to your team's proposal than I've given you. I appreciate your patience these last couple of days. It's been helpful to have the space to reflect on what I heard and gather some thoughts for you. I'm not going to beat around the bush, Elliot. Your strategy is not going to happen. Not because I didn't like it, but because it won't work. I asked Don's group a while ago to do some extensive research on an entry strategy to China and to assemble data on several segmented markets on the Pacific Rim. Once Alchatech announced its move into Asia, I knew we had to move quickly. Elliot, I know your people have worked hard for many years to get us established in Asia. There may be all kinds of reasons explaining why

we've never gotten there, but the bottom line is, we need to act now. We don't have the luxury of more false starts. I do want you involved intimately in getting us into Asia, Elliot. And I will rely heavily on you and your team to help us succeed there. I want you to come to Chicago in the next couple of weeks—"

Elliot interrupted Nancy, clearly livid. The muscles in his face were fully tensed. "Just how long ago did your little project start, Nancy?"

She knew the answer to this question was really going to set him off.

"About three months ago."

"*What?!* And when the hell were you planning on telling me? You could have saved me and my team months of work. If I'd known I was just wasting my time, and their time, I would have had them work on something else. And what am I supposed to tell them now? Why did you sit through that entire presentation the other day letting us all think you were supporting our work when you had every intention of just pulling the rug out from under us? Do you have any idea how many hours they put into that bloody presentation? And now you just waltz in here and announce that the entire time we were working on this, you were off doing your own thing? What the hell were you thinking, Nancy?"

By the time he finished, his voice had gotten pretty loud. Nancy never took raised voices well, especially from men. She raised hers back.

"Elliot, just who in the hell do you think you're talking to? Don't lecture me on how hard you and your people work. The painful truth is that you and your team have tried three times in the last four years to attempt a successful entry into Asia, all of which have failed miserably, to the tune of more than twenty million dollars of capital investment. And I don't know where you got your data from, but half of your assumptions about the market are completely off base. Nobody asked you to put together that extravaganza you paraded out the other day, and I don't even want to know how much you must have spent on that. So don't blame me for the disappointment you have to lay on them— you brought that on yourself. You blindsided me. You walked me into that conference room without any advance notice of what you were planning and expected me to just sit there looking calm and collected and then offer an enthusiastic thumbs up when they were all done. What the hell were *you* thinking, Elliot? Were you thinking about anything else but your own glory? Did you think about the fact that you might be setting them up for a huge fall if I didn't support the strategy? There are two sides to this story, Elliot. Don't try and lay this mess all at my feet."

Inside, Nancy couldn't believe the conversation had deteriorated so far, so fast. She clearly had underestimated how angry Elliot would be, but her ego wasn't ready to own her part of the failure. At least not yet.

Elliot headed down the martyr path next, getting up and pacing around the room. He was loud and intense as he said, "Nancy, I have done more for this organization in five years than anyone else in any other region. Australia wasn't even a blip on the radar before I got here. So don't throw money in my face, Nancy. We've wasted far more money on initiatives much less strategic than an entire market—the value of which is enormous compared to whatever pittance we'd spend to get there. Hell, how much did we lose in Toronto? We got massacred there. And have you gotten everything you've done in your career right on the first try? Are you going to sit there and tell me you've never failed at something big? Should I remind you of the second release of Paragon Global? You bet the farm on that being our premier high-end product, but it flopped and had to go back to the lab for retooling before it ever hit the streets. But we stuck with it, Nancy. And how much did that drain from the bottom line? And I backed you harder than anyone else when others were out to sabotage it. Sure, eventually it was a great success, but that's not how it started.

"So don't rub my nose in how many times we've failed, Nancy. We've all failed and spent big money doing it. If you want to throw money in my face, let's look at the margins I've delivered in the last two years. You held up Australia to the board at the last annual meeting as your victory trophy, gave me an honorable mention, and I just smiled and let you enjoy the glory. If I was out for my own personal glory, do you really think I'd be working at Brookreme? Sun and Cisco have both been knocking at my door offering up much bigger opportunities than this place. If glory was what I wanted, I'd have bailed long before now. But I happen to care about this place. I want to see us all succeed; I'm not just out to notch my atlas and indulge my own whims for the hell of it. For crying out loud, give me more credit than that."

Nancy stared down at her notebook in silent disbelief. She couldn't believe she had spoken to a valued colleague so disrespectfully, and frankly, she couldn't believe he'd done the same to her. She feared the worst—that she was about to lose an important leader and esteemed comrade.

Elliot stared out the window at the view of the water. For some reason, his mind flashed back to his first day at Brookreme, and the welcome party the Australian team gave him. There were only twenty-six on staff then. Now there were more than seventy. He had genuinely loved riding the wave of growth his region had enjoyed these past few years. He wondered if the wave had just crested.

After a few moments of very tense silence, Nancy knew she had to try and pull this conversation out of the fire somehow, though she wasn't sure if that was even possible. "Look, Elliot," she began, with a hint of a crack in her voice, "of all the ways I would have wanted this conversation to go, this is the last place I imagined us winding up. I don't know what to say. But I'll start by saying I'm sorry. I should never have said those things. There's no excuse. You are a talented leader, and I am very thankful for all you have done for Brookreme. I hope . . . I hope you know how much I value you as a colleague . . . and friend. And I'm sorry for not letting you into the conversation sooner on what Chicago has been up to with Asia. The last thing I wanted was to burst your team's bubble. I know you've worked hard, and I know you all want to succeed. I don't know how this got so out of hand . . . I'm just . . . sorry."

Elliot didn't respond right away. He wondered if she was really sincere, or just apologizing to try and avoid having him quit. It wasn't her style to be disingenuous, but it wasn't like her to be nasty either. He stared at her for a moment, then looked away. It seemed uncharacteristic that he had nothing to say. It was, however, quite characteristic of Nancy not to be able to endure the silence. So she broke the ice again.

"I can only guess what you must be thinking right now, Elliot. Whatever it is, please tell me. I don't want to fly back to Chicago leaving this unresolved. I know there is a lot more we have to talk about, and I want to do that without yelling at each other. You and I have worked out our differences before and our relationship did fine. I'd like to think we can do that now, even though it feels like a much bigger impasse than we've faced before." She waited and hoped he would respond. He did.

"Nancy, I know you didn't come all the way down here just to piss off my team and alienate me. I just need you to appreciate the awkward position this puts me in. I guess I need to own my part too. I never should have assumed your support of our proposal would be a slam dunk and let you walk into a meeting unprepared for what happened. I blew that. When Jim said you wanted to talk about Asia, I just wanted to believe you were giving us another shot. I shouldn't have assumed that. Regardless of how we got here, I now have a whole team of leaders who are going to feel used and led on. I don't know how I'm going to talk my way out of this one. Remember, you get to leave for Chicago today. I have to stay and face them. So where do we go from here?"

Nancy was relieved—at least she and Elliot were talking now. She didn't have any simple answers for him, but at least he was somewhat reengaged.

"Well, Elliot, I honestly do want you to come to Chicago, and perhaps bring a couple of your folks with you. I don't want to speak for Don's team. I want you to hear firsthand what they've learned. It's actually pretty amazing stuff. Once you hear their analysis, I think it will broaden your perspective. And I want your team to partner with the Chicago team on implementation. At the end of the day, your people are going to have to own those markets. I want you to see Chicago as a partner, not as a headquarters team swooping in to take over. I will help you clean up any mess with your team here. If they want to talk with me directly after they hear from you, I will make that happen. I don't want them thinking in any way that I'm not behind them, or worse, that I'm not behind you. I want your region to know I am personally committed to their success. I mean that."

Elliot knew she did. He wasn't necessarily feeling better. He knew the conversation with his team was going to be pretty rough. But he did feel like his relationship with Nancy would survive this. He accepted her invitation to come to Chicago. And he let her know that she had his commitment to do whatever was necessary to succeed in Asia this time around.

"I know I've let you down before in Asia, Nancy," he said. "This time, you have my word that we'll get it done. I think you and I still have some stuff we have to resolve between us. But like you said, we've done it before. And it probably won't be the last time. I guess what really counts is coming back to the table."

Elliot walked her down to the car to see her off. There was a lot of regard conveyed in all that was unspoken on the quiet walk out to the car. But Nancy felt like this time she'd been lucky, and that luck came at the price of a hard lesson. It was an awkward goodbye, but she did give him a hug.

On the flight home, she reflected on how many times she'd had conversations with people, in a sincere effort to make them feel included, but had led them on to believe they were involved to a degree they really were not. She also reflected on times in her career that it had happened to her, and how lousy it felt. She'd never wanted to make anyone feel like that, and here she was on the other side of the table. One thing was clear to her. This was one predicament she would exert all her will to never be in again.

For the Moments Yet to Come . . .

1. With what aspects of control do you struggle? How does your struggle show up in your relationships with those you lead?

2. How have you manipulated others into thinking their voice was more included than perhaps you truly intended for it to be? What was your rationale for doing so?

3. What experiences have you had of offering your input when asked for it, only to later realize that it wasn't really wanted? How did you feel?

4. What voices do you need to invite around your table more than they are there today?

5. What results could your organization achieve that it isn't achieving today if a greater degree of people's passion were to be unleashed?

CHAPTER FOUR

AN IMAGINATIVE DREAM

The Death of Monotony, The Dare of Dreaming

Dreams are answers to questions we haven't yet figured out how to ask.

Fox Mulder, *The X-Files*

Opportunity: Dream first, set targets later, to push leaders to the limits of their capability.

Got exasperation?

The annual email from HR arrived to its usual welcome—rolling eyes, huffy sighs, moans, snickering, and Dilbert-esque mockery.

————————

To: All Department Heads
From: Anita
Subject: BPAP

It's that time of year again, everyone—time for performance planning! I know we're all eager to see the final numbers on the merit pool and get increases processed. Let's get those goals set and those evaluations submitted on time to your respective HR leads, and we'll make sure we get our part done. I've attached new templates for this year which include the redefined rating categories for your people. As you look at the new templates, please remember

- No more than 10 percent of your folks can be rated "high potential." You must include a hi-po development plan and three-year career outlook in the evaluation for every person you put in the "high potential" category.

- If you have people in the "deficient performance" category, you must include documentation on performance counseling sessions in their evaluations. You also need to include your HR lead in evaluation meetings with people in this category, and get the employee's signature on the form at the end of the meeting.
- If you have people in the "deficient performance" category for a second consecutive year, you also need to include *both* documentation on performance counseling sessions and the transition exit strategy with the evaluation. Again, you need to include the HR lead in the evaluation meeting and get the employee's signature on the form.

We're hoping the new online input screens will greatly streamline this process, leaving more time for coaching. I'd suggest you refer to the training manual if you have any questions about how to determine performance ratings. Please feel free to reach out to your HR leads if you need additional help. Thanks in advance for making the Brookreme Performance Acceleration Process (BPAP) a key part of shaping our culture and driving Brookreme's success.

———

"Key part, my ass," mumbled Sara to herself. "The only thing driving results around here are us leprechauns making all the magic happen. This crap only gets in the way. Instead of getting ready for the next Asia summit, they want me to write out a bunch of stupid goals that have nothing to do with how I'll spend the next twelve months, look grateful when I'm handed my whopping 2.8 percent raise (which means zilch after taxes), act like I feel all honored when I'm told I'm a high-potential, and then go back to life as usual. I mean, what the hell?" On either side of Sara's workspace, you could hear her colleagues mumbling pretty much the same things to themselves as they all received Anita's memo.

Sara was Brookreme's notoriously sassy marketing whiz-kid. Most enjoyed working with her because of her refreshing, albeit unpolished, tell-it-like-it-is candor. Her ideas had led to some of Brookreme's most successful marketing campaigns as well as some of their high-margin bundled solutions. If anybody was a "high potential" up-and-comer, it was Sara.

She reported directly to Nolan, Brookreme's chief marketing officer. Nolan was an institution at Brookreme—one of the few remaining people who had been with the company since the beginning. He had cut his teeth at a top-notch

Madison Avenue agency, and he brought a deep understanding of the more sophisticated approaches to using strategic marketing for driving revenue growth and market share. Nolan was not an inspirational leader with a passion to be at the cutting edge, but he didn't pretend to be. He knew his field and he knew his company, both inside and out. Many in the organization respected that and considered Nolan both an important asset and a critical part of Brookreme's living memory of how it rose to become a successful organization. Others thought Nolan was more of a relic than an icon—one who would eventually find his way into Nancy's sights when she next took aim. A few wondered why he'd survived this long.

Nolan himself wasn't worried about his job. He knew Nancy valued his perspective. She wasn't looking for him to be the silver-bullet answer man, because she believed Brookreme's future was more about innovative products and world-class services than marketing strategy. Nolan's presence was more or less benign to Nancy, and they both liked it that way.

Nolan and Sara often drove each other nuts, though. She was a creative genius, he was a deliberate process expert. Her hundred-mile-an-hour approach to life, her ability to produce ideas faster than anyone could ever implement them, and her imaginative energy inspired others, but rendered her impulsive and reckless in Nolan's eyes. Nolan, on the other hand, was slow and cautious to a fault from Sara's perspective. "If he were any slower, he'd lapse into a coma," she'd commonly grumble.

This would be Sara's third year through the BPAP reporting to Nolan, and if she heard the words "honor the process" even once, she feared she would lose it. Wearing the title of "high potential" meant little to Sara. All she saw was the chance to attend more meetings that Nancy spoke at, which was hardly her lifelong ambition. A lot of young leaders with impressive track records had experienced a meteoric rise to exciting opportunities at Brookreme, and Sara couldn't understand why her star hadn't risen further. She had become increasingly cynical over the past three years and had grown to feel that Nolan was actively holding her back.

Sara had come to Don's notice, and some of the strategic insights Don had impressed Nancy with had actually come from Sara's work. Don wanted Sara on the Asia team, and Nolan was glad to give her a shot at stepping up. Unfortunately, Nolan missed the opportunity to mark this appointment as the beginning of the next phase of Sara's career at Brookreme, which is what it really was. Instead, he simply left Sara a voice mail to attend the next Asia meeting the day before it took place.

Sara was genuinely excited about Asia. She had some great ideas and she knew it. But in her cynicism she interpreted the last-minute feel of Nolan's voice mail as meaning the assignment was the usual punishment for being good—a heavier workload.

Sara logged onto the Brookreme intranet and pulled up the BPAP screen. As she read the words "insert goals with metrics and timelines here" she let out an exasperated sigh. She could hear Nolan's drone as he reviewed the performance plan with her, almost like an annoying song that she couldn't get out of her head: "Now, Sara, tell me exactly how you intend to measure this goal . . . That's interesting, but I'm not sure we'll have the resources to accomplish that this year . . . you should use the existing processes and tools we've put in place to get that done . . . you can't do this all by yourself . . . you need to involve the sales organization and the field for this . . ." Blah, blah, blah. As she worked her way through the form, she imagined herself saying, "Gosh, Nolan, should I set a goal for how many times a day I'll go to the bathroom?" Or, "Hey, Nolan, I have an idea—let's create a process for how we create processes, and let's measure how well our measurement is working. I could spend six months writing the manuals and designing the three-day training program for a national rollout, and we could make it one of my top goals. Then, next year, you could label me high-potential again, give me a big 2 percent raise, and we'll pretend that I actually added significant value when we both know I didn't do jack! Doesn't that sound exciting?"

Sara knew she was impatient, and even though she loathed bureaucracy she realized that some processes and procedures were necessary. Some days she even felt Nolan wasn't such a bad guy. But she hated feeling like she had to check her soul at the door to talk about goals that felt completely disconnected from what she could really be successful doing for Brookreme. Being the quick thinker that she was, her frustration began to change into something else in her agile mind. What if Nolan could somehow live the excruciating monotony of Sara's experience? What if there was a way for her to really push her own limits, and Brookreme's, in this evaluation conversation without having Nolan react in his usual sickeningly paternalistic and condescending way? As she began to type, a faint mischievous grin emerged at one corner of her mouth. . . .

For the Moment

What do you expect from Sara in her meeting with Nolan?

What biases do you have about Sara? From where might they originate?

How might you counsel her to prepare for the meeting?

How could Nolan use the meeting for the benefit of both Sara and the organization?

If you've been part of any organization that's attempted to create processes and systems in the service of efficiency and standardization, you know Sara's pain all too well. And you know Nolan's. Standardization and efficiency are essential elements of helping a complex organization hit peak stride. Any economies of scale, beyond their value in dollars and cents, should free up intellectual capacity to continually improve performance. But all too often, intransigent devotion to systems and processes anesthetizes people's creative impulses and numbs their hope for reaching greater individual frontiers. Needless to say, that wasn't the original intent.

> *I saw—with shut eyes, but acute mental vision—I saw the pale student of unhallowed arts kneeling beside the thing he had put together. I saw the hideous phantasm of a man stretched out, and then, on the working of some powerful engine, show signs of life and stir with an uneasy, half-vital motion. Frightful must it be, for supremely frightful would be the effect of any human endeavor to mock the stupendous mechanism of the Creator of the world.*
> MARY WOLLSTONECRAFT SHELLEY
> *Intoduction to* Frankenstein

CORPORATE FRANKENSTEIN: THE MAKING OF A MONSTER

The explosion of enterprise-wide technologies intended to help manage complexity and streamline processes through the '80s and '90s fueled amazing new levels of efficiency and standardization.

Enterprise resource planning (ERP) software has reached an incredible level of sophistication, facilitating the integration of all functional departments into one enterprise-wide system. The software packages that knit sales, delivery, billing, production, inventory management, quality management, and human resource management into a cross-functional whole are the biggest and most complex available commercially. In fact, the fourth largest software company in the world is SAP, which focuses exclusively on ERPs. Organizations from software vendors and hospitals to manufacturing industries and even government departments have adopted ERPs, and in many cases the results were stunning: waste and redundancy were slashed and productivity went way up. Not surprisingly, organizations went on bureaucracy-busting safaris, hunting down every possible duplicative, valueless, or needlessly manual task that could be eliminated or simplified.

Unfortunately, the process-improvement bureaucracy that was created to eliminate the rest of the bureaucracy has created a new set of frustrations. Most notoriously, it often squelches a leader's capacity to dream. Leaders become mindlessly devoted to compliance with these processes, and they condition those they lead to do the same. In so doing, they unintentionally neuter imagination throughout the organization.

GE's famous "Workout Sessions" of the late '80s heralded a new way for the world to get the work out of the organization. Today, Six Sigma is taking organizations by storm with its sharp focus on high-precision measurement, defect elimination, and cost containment. Originally, Six Sigma was the idea that there should be no more than 3.4 defects per million parts produced by any manufacturing or process stream. Today, Six Sigma has become the notion that you pursue customer satisfaction and producer efficiency to the precise point at which greater quality is not cost-effective. Motorola developed and trademarked the idea, but the methods they employed have been adapted by many large companies, including GE, Honeywell, Ford, Raytheon, and Microsoft.

Since we're talking about corporate monsters here, let me make one thing perfectly clear: the performance gains we get from things like SAP, Six Sigma, and many other kinds of technologies are fantastic. The ability to measure the value of important activity and have available data in near-real-time to shorten feedback loops and cycle times and ultimately increase tight margins has enabled great advances in manufacturing, marketing, and customer service. But with these advances have come hidden costs that may not be fully appreciated. Taking these measurement and process management tools to an extreme, leaders leave little room for participants to dream imaginatively about the future of the organization, to conceive it in ways beyond what can be envisioned in the current form. More fundamentally, it stifles leaders' ability to dream about their *own* capabilities beyond where they are today.

How does this happen? Think about an ERP like SAP. The software alone costs millions of dollars to buy, frequently takes years to implement, and changes the work processes of every function in the organization. Of course, if an ERP is not implemented properly, you run the risk of paralyzing the company's functions. With the stakes this high, the senior leadership team pays the bills to the software company and the consultants and tells employees to do exactly—and I mean *exactly*—what the implementation manual says. The resulting regime is frequently so systematic—or even robotic—that creativity is often suffocated, and "skunk works" projects—the notorious nickname for unsanctioned, politically risky initiatives—are kept underground, off the radar of the mainstream organization. In reality, such endeavors should be front and center, enjoying the excitement of the organization for the potential they promise. But the political and social penalties for deviating from predictable, controlled procedure are too strong for people who would otherwise bring exciting dreams to the table. So they share them judiciously, in whispered conversations behind closed doors—or, worse, keep them to themselves.

Ironically, these outcomes are a perverted deviation from the results these managerial advances intended. W. Edwards Deming, considered by many as the father of the Quality Management movement in the United States, argued in his 1986 manifesto, *Out of the Crisis,* that quality was in fact meant to be in the service of innovation. Deming said:

"One requirement for innovation is faith that there will be a future. Innovation, the foundation of the future, cannot thrive unless top management have declared unshakable commitment to quality . . . until then . . . everyone else in the company will be skeptical about the effectiveness of their best efforts."

In other words, improving quality through process and measurement should *propel* innovation, not *asphyxiate* it.

The paradoxical tension between standardization and innovation is one most leaders struggle to live with. Highly entrepreneurial leaders pride themselves on the freedom to be opportunistic and wear their disdain for bureaucracy on their sleeves, yet are pained by their lack of effectiveness in getting even the most basic things done. "Everything is chaos" is the cry in such environments. By contrast, leaders in well-honed process organizations competing in mature markets tout their precision with great pride, showing impressive Gantt charts and bar graphs boasting world-class levels of efficiency and standardization. Of course, leaders in these environments often lament, "Innovation isn't in our DNA." By default, innovation and well-organized process appear to have unnecessarily become an either/or choice.

I believe you can have excellence in both without compromise. Innovation and standardization can cohabit synergistically in the same organization, even one whose primary competitive basis is cost and speed. In fact, I would say that for twenty-first-century competitive performance, they must. But first we need to understand why they collide so frequently.

> *Know your limitations and be content with them.*
> *Too much ambition results in a promotion to a job you*
> *can't do.*
> DAVID BRENT, *regional manager* WERNHAM HOGG
> *The Office*

THE SYSTEMATIC NEUTERING OF IMAGINATION

The pain of process and standardization choking innovation, and the capacity to dream outside the boundaries of convention, have both become vividly apparent in the pharmaceutical industry. Big pharma has invested heavily in the R&D technologies necessary to scale clinical trials and compound modeling to impressive degrees. This allows for a development pipeline of many compounds simultaneously and also facilitates clinical trials of multiple compounds across a variety of therapeutic areas. Oncology can be testing their compounds at the same time cardiovascular, metabolic diseases, and neurosciences are all testing theirs. But the industry has come under heavy scrutiny for its inability to contain the extreme costs associated with bringing a blockbuster drug to market, which can sometimes take up to twelve years. A 2002 article by Gautam Naik in the *Wall Street Journal* reported:

"In 2000, U.S. drug makers together spent more than $25 billion on R&D, but filed fewer than 150 applications for new drugs. In 1983, they spent less than $4 billion and filed more than 250 applications. Companies such as AstraZeneca PLC, Schering-Plough Corp., Merck & Co., and others, all face imminent patent expirations on blockbuster drugs which typically account for a large proportion of a drug maker's profit."

While big American pharma companies rely heavily on being able to cash in on the blockbuster drugs they patent, consumers and employers alike are desperate to curtail skyrocketing prescription drug costs. As Marialba Martinez said in the *Puerto Rico Herald:*

"Because generic drugs can be up to 70 percent cheaper than brand-name drugs, they sell only $11.1 billion a year—less than 10 percent of the total $132.1 billion annual drug sales market—but account for 45 percent of all prescriptions filled in the U.S."

This puts big pharma in a double bind: it is increasingly costly to develop and bring to market new blockbusters, and consumers are eager to find ways to reach generic alternatives.

But pharma companies face a problem even bigger than development cost or fighting off generics—they face an astonishing lack of results. While you would expect there to be a substantial dropout rate of potential products as they make their way through the R&D pipeline, and the termination of compounds with little promise long before scaling them to clinical trials, still, there seems to be a disproportionate lack of commercialized innovation from these mega R&D processes relative to the sizeable investments. Why is that? A closer look at the environments in which these products are birthed is revealing.

In most R&D environments, especially those of a complex scientific nature, product development cycles are measured in years. The conflict with the commercialization processes, whose time horizons are measured more in months, can be intractable. Hundreds of millions of dollars are being invested in compounds presenting the greatest promise to return billions of dollars of revenue and shareholder value. The cost pressure in such environments is astronomical. The presumption is that the greater the degree of scalable standardization, the less the cost of the development. To exacerbate this pressure, the commercialization people are clamoring to get the product launched. One day of delay in a product launch can equal more than a million dollars of lost revenue for a blockbuster drug. The paradox to be managed is that the process of innovation is anything but linear.

The greatest, most pioneering drugs are often discovered in areas outside the therapeutic arena in which the development was targeted. Dr. George Nicholas Papanicolaou's chance observation, while doing a genetic study, of cancer cells on a slide containing a specimen from a woman's uterus spawned the routine use of the Pap smear, a simple test that has saved millions of women from the ravages of cervical cancer. Viagra (Sildenafil) began its journey as a cardiovascular drug for hypertension, but due to a chance side effect during clinical trials, it was found to be effective at treating erectile dysfunction (and ineffective at treating angina, its original intended use). Even the dreaded Thalidomide, once used to treat morning sickness in pregnant women but withdrawn after causing horrible birth defects, is now a promising treatment for multiple melanoma, an incurable cancer.

The very nature of the experimentation process, especially when researchers are trying to understand the impact of a drug on a living organism, is ultimately about betting against extremely long odds. Innovation happens largely from opportunism, chance, and atypical reading of scientific data returning from animals—or in later clinical trials from humans. Being overly opportunistic and imprudent in the pursuit of groundbreaking medicines is simply too costly. Being inflexibly regimented in the approach risks missing the very opportunities being pursued. As a result, researchers are too steeped in one hypothesis to deviate from it long enough to see fresh perspectives. Striking the right balance between both is the aim.

If one advances confidently in the direction of his dreams, and endeavors to live the life which he has imagined, he will meet with a success unexpected in common hours.

HENRY DAVID THOREAU

DESIRE IS THE FUEL OF DREAMS

Dr. Beth Seidenberg, named to *Fortune* magazine's Top Five Women to Watch list in October 2004, is one of the pharmaceutical and biotech industry's most gifted drug developers. Having brought a record forty-plus products through FDA registration, she is one of the most talented and passionate leaders I've had the privilege to work with. Everything about her work is infused by a passion to bring good medicines to patients who need them. Every product she has touched has a dream behind it of enhancing the lives of people suffering with complex diseases. When she arrived at Amgen, the world's largest biotech company, as head of global development and chief medical officer, they had two products in their portfolio, the most recent of which had come to market ten years earlier. Three years after her arrival, under her leadership, they had six new major products on the market. Her desire to see innovative products make a worldwide difference in disease areas in which existing medicines are falling short served as the foundation of her work. Today, she is a partner at Kleiner Perkins Caufield & Byers, one of the world's premier venture capital firms, helping identify and fund the most promising and cutting-edge medical advances that exist. This is what Beth says about her work:

> I come to work every day and ask myself, "Where are there needs in health care and how can the products I am developing or pursuing change the practice of medicine?"
>
> That has always been the guiding principle of hiring people, making decisions on products, choosing strategy. I start with the end in mind. Where is this going to take you ten years from now? For example, what if you had products that didn't require bringing patients into the clinic once a week, but could still improve their quality of life, their disease outcome, which in turn would lead to improvements in their workplaces? These are the questions that push the boundaries of convention.
>
> Innovators need to create environments where people are naturally proactive in product development. You have to get people to ask the right questions and challenge the existing norms and assumptions about how things are done—with the regulator, the physician, the manufacturers, etc. You put yourself in a position where it's

acceptable—expected—to ask the harder questions. I would sit with teams, talking with the FDA, the CMS, and try and set the example. I would ask the hard questions, "Could we try . . ." or "I know the regulations say this, but have we thought about . . ." People need to see that bad things don't happen by pushing the envelope. When people are afraid and a lack of experience holds them back, innovation is hard to foster.

My role has always been to give teams the confidence they need, and take their deep technical knowledge and leverage it while at the same time challenging their assumptions. It's magic when it happens. I remember going to the FDA and changing a dose based on pharmacokinetic modeling. That created a market opportunity that didn't exist [before].

Part of not squashing innovation is never assuming the obvious is obvious to the person on the other side of the table. Just because the FDA has seen cardio toxicity 100 times doesn't mean you can skip the underpinnings of your logic. You need to always demonstrate your grounding in deep technical excellence when pushing the boundaries of convention.

Innovation has to recognize and honor that there are different types of people in organizations. Operational and process folks, who keep things on track, safe, in control and compliance, must be *equally* as honored and celebrated as those idea generators getting great results in their clinical trials. Both must be celebrated well, but an organization can never lose sight of respecting they are different people. Their risk and discipline tolerances are different. They think differently. They see different things. At the *intersection* of their differences is the greatest value of innovation.

The implications for corporate processes are clear, regardless of industry. The natural tensions between process efficiency and dreaming imaginatively must be traversed to ensure that neither is compromised. This is easier said than done, to be sure.

The Worst Offender

Perhaps no part of corporate life is more imagination-killing than the notorious "performance management" process. It's painfully ironic that a process intended to liberate the highest levels of performance from people has, for many organizations, become one of the most dreaded, monotonous, disconnected-from-reality experiences people have in the workplace. Although I have seen a number of organizations employ this process quite effectively, too many have gone astray in their attempts to connect people and performance. According to a 2004 survey by the Hudson Employment Index, though two-thirds of U.S. workers are very or somewhat satisfied with their compensation and benefits, many feel their organizations apply inconsistent standards to setting pay levels and managing employee performance. One-third of the workforce surveyed reported being unsure about the review criteria. A majority of workers (60 percent) indicated that, despite performance management processes, simple tenure determined pay where they worked, and just 35 percent believed that actual performance was a more important deciding factor. Further, 31 percent reported that their company did not have a consistent standard or process to determine employee compensation, which may explain why only half believed that they were paid on par with their peers.

Here's how performance reviews work in many organizations. I've actually seen what I'm about to describe—and you probably have too. You approach the experience with all the desire you'd have for a root canal. Basically, you write a set of goals for your boss or, worse, get handed a set of goals by your boss. The goals have some contrived metrics that routinely have no relevance to how you spend your days. Then, at the end of the year, the boss goes around and talks to people about what you accomplished and assembles a set of feedback to give you about the goals you set out to achieve. The data are often a surprise, and you hear for the first time from anonymous sources (usually easily detected) about problematic behavior that could have been shared months earlier. Then you get an insipid rating classifying you into some category with others in the organization—often a category kept secret from you. Peter Block, in his timeless book, *Stewardship: Choosing Service Over Self-Interest,* says eloquently:

"The belief that performance can be induced through coercion in the form of measurement is one of the roots of the problem [self-interest] we are trying to solve, and using tighter controls in the name of improvement is trying to cure ourselves by injecting larger doses of the virus causing the disease . . . What truly matters in our lives is measured through conversation."

Most performance measurement today, or at least the "documentation" of performance, feels more motivated by litigation-avoidance than performance-enriching intentions. In my experience, far more attention gets paid to documenting performance problems of employees likely to be fired than ever gets paid to the marvelous contributions of the most gifted employees. When's the last time you heard someone express enthusiastic anticipation of their performance review meeting? The discussion that should be generating the greatest amount of desire and dreams has become a discussion for producing high levels of anxiety, apathy, and resentment—far from the conditions necessary for big dreams.

Desire, not precision, is at the heart of dreams. A leader's ability to conceive of a future, of something *more,* is predicated first on her *desire* for more. Her ability to reach that destination could well require a healthy degree of process efficiency, but dreaming of that place is initially born of her desire for it.

In contrast to many incumbent leaders, emerging leaders tend to dream big. Their disenfranchisement often propels them toward a passionate desire for great change. Sometimes their desire creates delusions of grandeur and spawns arrogance. Nonetheless, their ability to conceive of an exciting future can be inspiring. In my research with emerging leaders, the most energizing, hopeful conversations were anchored in dreaming. They cherish the invitation to dream, and it is obvious in their stories:

- "I talked with a leader once about his dreams for our organization. We were able to 'dream together and dream big.' It was a great conversation, and when it came time to actually do the work, I was able to jump in with both feet and exercise some leadership within the dreaming."
- "Conversations that are most powerful are ones that instill a hope or dream that can be realized in my life and my work. Those conversations are a catalyst for the desire and action to see the hope of a dream lived out. I'm in one of the conversations right now with my leader, mentor, and friend. We're discussing the direction and vision of our organization, and it is such an honor to know that my opinion matters."
- "Recently I scheduled some time with a leader to go over some dreams that I had about an upcoming project. Not only did he

get behind what I was doing, but he began to dream with me, using contacts, ideas, and his own passions. When I went into his office, I felt like I had a good idea which I was relatively excited about. When I left, I felt like it was an incredible idea that we could both share in . . . and the scope of the project was expanded beyond my original dreaming."

An imaginative dream is an invaluable asset to any heart—and any organization. The poet and diarist Anaïs Nin once wrote, "The dream was always running ahead of me. To catch up, to live for a moment in unison with it, that was the miracle." All of us want to catch up to our dreams. Emerging leaders believe they actually can. The raw power of desire, coupled with an imaginative dream and informed by the wisdom, knowledge, and patience of a willing, seasoned leader, can propel the next generation of leadership into the miraculous.

For the Moment

How recently have you practiced the art of dreaming?

How recently have you heard—truly heard—about someone else's dreams?

Do you have a story of a dream you've caught up to, or want to catch up with?

WHEN ORDINARY PEOPLE DREAM

Most people want to cheer when Dorothy Boyd, the "you had me at hello" character played by Renée Zellweger in the movie *Jerry Maguire,* gets up from her desk, packs up her things, declares, "I just want to be inspired," then walks out to pursue that inspiration in a high-risk venture with Jerry. Her defiance of the small-minded politics and soul-numbing monotony in which she'd been working is one many leaders in organizations fantasize about having the courage to express. She sees passion and integrity in Jerry, and she bets her future on it. Most employees in organizations are longing for leaders to unshackle them in the same way. They have dreams for themselves and their organizations—dreams to make great contributions, to achieve. Standing between their private dreams and the guts to pursue those dreams might be a leader holding them captive through unbending devotion to lifeless procedures, or a leader capable of setting them free—enabled by helpful process—to make the difference they've long imagined making.

Everyone loves the story of a dark horse—the one who defies the odds, comes from behind, perseveres against enormous obstacles, scorns the mockery of naysayers, privately writhes in anguish and fear, and ultimately triumphs in achievement of something great and near-impossible. What's interesting is why we love these stories. Personally, I think it's because we all have a dark horse inside of us. We all secretly imagine ourselves accepting an Oscar, kissing the World Cup trophy, walking a red carpet of camera flashes, taking a bow before millions as the gold medal is hung around our neck, being lifted into the air and carried around the field by the team, or having our name carved into a plaque for all to see. Admit it. You too have grabbed your hairbrush in the privacy of your room and transformed it into a microphone, belting out whatever song was blasting at the moment. You too have secretly written that acceptance speech and delivered it—maybe even out loud! You've done it because you have the capacity to dream. This doesn't necessarily mean that you have some pathological, narcissistic streak or that your ego and vanity are out of control. It's because you, like everyone, imagine yourself and your life as *more*. You want your own natural gifts rooted within you to blossom, to the amazement of the world around you.

The dark horse captivates us. It's woven into our national culture. It's easiest perhaps to recognize a dark horse in sports, in which the metaphor of victory and defeat is played out regularly, publicly, and with great fanfare. The Olympic Games never fail to deliver on this promise. One of my favorite Olympics stories is that of Wilma Rudolph, whose story might have been remarkable enough given that her success came within the context of a segregated South. But her success was more astounding given the circumstances of her childhood. She was born the twentieth of twenty-two children. From an early age she suffered many illnesses, including double pneumonia, scarlet fever, and polio, losing the use of her left leg. She did not walk normally until the age of twelve, at which time she decided to become an athlete. She ran in her first Olympic Games only four years later. It wasn't until 1960, however, that she won three gold medals and established herself as the fastest woman in the world. Wilma's is a story rooted in the belief that dreams are more powerful than circumstance. "Doctors told me I would never walk again," she said. "My mother told me I would. I chose to believe my mother." As a result, she has become an icon for defying the odds and overcoming physical and social obstacles.

Big dreams come to life every day on the playing field and the big screen, and the corporate world has known countless stories of unexpected greatness as well. One of my favorites is the story of the minivan. Now a staple vehicle of American families coast to coast, the minivan was the brainchild of Hal Sperlich, a successful car designer with the Ford Motor Company. Sperlich had been part of the design team that launched the wildly successful Mustang in the mid-1960s. Sperlich warned his then boss, Henry Ford II, of the threat of the Japanese to American auto makers, but Ford stubbornly rejected Sperlich's ideas for more fuel-efficient vehicles.

The Japanese and other importers made substantial inroads during the 1970s, taking one-third of the American automobile market by 1982. The Big Three U.S. auto makers lost $15 billion; Ford and Chrysler struggled to survive. Sperlich and his friend Lee Iacocca had both been fired by Ford at this point, but were snapped up by Chrysler, which was relying on a U.S. government bailout to avoid bankruptcy and liquidation. Sperlich boosted Chrysler's existing K-car program into reality when he arrived there, and he used the K platform to spin off successful derivatives like the minivan, a Sperlich project that Henry Ford II had rejected. In only a few short years, the minivan became a million-vehicle market, with Chrysler owning fully half, thanks to Sperlich's vision and determination. It is not an exaggeration to say that Sperlich's design saved Chrysler from extinction.

> *We run, not because we think it is doing us good, but because we enjoy it and cannot help ourselves. The human spirit is indomitable.*
> SIR ROGER BANNISTER, *first man to run a sub-four-minute mile, on May 6, 1954*

The Bridge to Relationship: Letting Big Dreams Be the Impetus for Targets That Bring Leaders to New Heights

Dreaming isn't "touchy feely." It's powerful. In your own life, examine the places your passion has driven you to success that surprised you. Wasn't it a dream—even if you didn't name it as such—that propelled you? Process standardization and the creative impulses of innovators need never rival one another in unhealthy contention. Of course they will always be in tension. That tension is good. It forces inherent trade-offs to be understood and traversed from multiple vantage points. Too much of either poses substantial risk. In balance, incumbent and emerging leaders can find the wonderful economies of scale that process standardization offers and still enjoy the power that big dreams exert.

Here are some starter thoughts on how you might pursue that balance. Of course, please dream big to add more to the list.

1. *Be deliberate with what and how you measure.* As the adage goes, "what you expect, you inspect." An organization's metrics tell much about its culture and ethos. They shape behavior and beliefs. Most organizations collect far more data than they could ever apply to decision making. You only need a small, vital set of key metrics tied to your brand, your competitive positioning, your customer's responses to your offerings, and a few key initiatives. Make sure the data collection and use of metrics is fully transparent to the organization, especially those who have control over the outcomes.

2. *Be sure your process-improvement initiatives are generative.* Improving processes, standardizing practices across complex organizations is never a static activity. Processes, like other parts of a system, are living and organic. They need to re-create themselves perpetually to adapt to ever-changing conditions. Standardization, then, is never finished. It must have creativity built into it to ensure that it is a generative endeavor—continually innovating in the service of higher performance levels.

3. *Talk animatedly about your dreams.* Let those with whom you lead know what you dream for the organization. Use colorful language that

invites emotions and inspires imaginative aspirations in others. Let people know how your dreams benefit them, and invite them to help you realize them. Let others see how your dreams for the organization sustain you when your confidence flags.

4. *Know others' dreams and your part in realizing them.* Ask people, especially during any conversations about performance, what their dreams are. Yes, they may react to such an awkward question, but don't give up. Don't ask them for their personal vision statement, because that's what you'll get. Ask them for the dreams they have for what they hope to become in order to move the organization and their life forward.

5. *Set targets that make leaders stretch.* Undergirded by a dream, even the most daunting targets feel like an attractive challenge. People relish the chance to push away from what's known and comfortable into terrain that is unfamiliar, in the service of expanding their capacity. Once leaders' dreams are known, help them reach beyond what they might otherwise aspire to, and enjoy their surprise as they attain what they set out for.

6. *Celebrate dreams come true.* Never underestimate the power of a standing ovation. When people realize a dream, or even a portion of a dream, it had to come at an impressive cost. Sacrifice. Risk. The pessimism of others. Personal doubt. Extraordinary relationships. Creativity. Determination. Regardless of where you fall in the picture, be assured the achievement is important to them. Stand up and cheer.

Let's go back to Brookreme and see how Sara fares in her performance planning and review conversation with Nolan. I'll give you fair warning now: all my fantasies for how I've long dreamed these meetings should go will inevitably spill out all over this conversation. Do me a favor. Dream with me. These are some of the most important conversations in which leaders engage. Why not dream about making them utterly fantastic experiences?

Sara arrived a bit early to Nolan's office for her meeting, which was scheduled to last about two hours. Nolan's door was closed, so she assumed he might be running behind in his current meeting. But at 2:00, Nolan emerged from the elevator with his coat on, carrying a shopping bag. When he reached the area outside his office, he smiled at Sara and motioned for her to come in. He gave his assistant an inquisitive look, nodding toward his door, and in return she said, "Yep, everything is all set—just the way you wanted it." Nolan simply said, "That's great, thanks." He opened the door and gestured for Sara to enter in front of him, chivalrous man that he was. Sara strode in and assumed they would be sitting at Nolan's small conference table. But two steps in, she stopped and noticed the table had been moved to the center of the room. Not only had it been moved, but it was set with fresh linens, and next to it was a rolling buffet cart with chafing dishes containing a hot meal.

Nolan walked past Sara, lifted the lids off the warming dishes, and said, "If I recall, you are a fan of Chilean sea bass."

Sara was dumbfounded. She looked at him and simply said, "Uh, yeah, I am. What is all this, Nolan?"

Nolan began to serve the food on the china, bearing Brookreme's corporate logo, that had been given to them by one of their clients who manufactured fine bone china. He motioned for Sara to take a seat.

"Well, I got your email on Monday, and it really made me think. So first, let me say thanks for sending it. Your point about these conversations being full of anxiety and awkwardness and your hopes that maybe this one could be something more jump-started my marketing mind. I thought to myself, *When I was back on Madison Avenue, we pulled out all the stops when a really important client came in for a meeting. We treated them like royalty because clients were everything in that world.* I remembered how fun it was to see their faces when they felt treated well. It didn't matter what the conversation was—good news, bad news, brainstorming, creative presen-tations, whatever—they always went better—you know, felt friendlier—over a great meal. It occurred to me that, in some ways, you are my client. Your ability to contribute to Brookreme, to accomplish the things we've asked of you, and your willingness to be open to new challenges, is probably directly predicated on your feeling my support and advocacy. So, drawing on my past life, I decided, what the hell, I'll give it a shot. So, I hope you feel when this conversation is over that—how did you put it?" Nolan picked up Sara's printed email from his desk and read the part he'd highlighted: "'You see me more than as a cog in your wheel, that my hopes matter, that I have dreams I want to pursue too, and that sometimes conventional approaches to important conversations can turn the magnificent into the mundane.'

You always were good with a turn of phrase, Sara. I want you to know your hopes matter to me, and to Brookreme. I want you to feel this conversation as magnificent."

Sara could hardly speak. She stared at Nolan as if he'd just arrived from outer space. Her silence had Nolan a tad worried, and he swallowed hard. He genuinely wanted this to go well, and he hoped it hadn't tanked out of the gate.

"Holy shit!" is all Sara could muster.

They both laughed.

Nolan said, "Is that good?"

"Hell, yeah, it's good," Sara replied. "I just never thought . . . I mean, I wasn't really sure if . . . well, you know . . . my email . . . I didn't know if it would piss you off or what. I mean, c'mon, Nolan, this isn't exactly your style. No offense or anything, but I'm sure you can appreciate this isn't exactly what I expected. I'm kind of overwhelmed, really."

Nolan laughed again. "I may be capable of more surprises than you give me credit for, Sara."

"I guess so!" She laughed, passing Nolan the basket of bread.

For the next few minutes, they just enjoyed their food, complimenting the caterer and commenting on the great flavors. After a while, Nolan shifted the conversation to the matter at hand. He reached over to his desk and got the file containing two copies of Sara's completed BPAP, to which he'd added his comments, and handed her a copy.

"So why don't we start with your thoughts on this past year. I was fascinated by your commentary, Sara, and appreciated your candor about what's been hard for you. Talking about *what* you worked on is simple. Helping me understand fully the *experience* of your work gives me a view into you and some ideas on how I can work toward making your experience this year even better. I only wish I'd known how frustrated you were juggling so many priorities. You are such a powerhouse of productivity, I guess it didn't occur to me you were struggling. You make it all look so easy. Tell me more about how the year was."

Sara didn't miss a beat. "Well, of course, for the most part it was a great year. Yeah, there were a few bumps that I wished hadn't been there, but that's Brookreme. We're always bumping into each other trying to get too much done. Everything is an urgent priority, right?"

Sara went on in her dynamic, vivacious way to talk about the projects that frustrated her, and of course, threw in a few choice colorful expressions. She spoke honestly about mistakes she'd made and when she'd planned her time poorly and missed some deadlines to which she'd committed. Sara hated missing any commitments and was pretty hard on herself for doing so. And she spoke with exuberance about what she loved about the year, highlighting the Asia project. She went on for the next twenty minutes about how she thought Brookreme had a shot at penetrating Asia with great success this time because they had really done their homework, studied the Chinese technology growth, and spotted some trends in a few submarket segments she was sure Alchatech was clueless about. She knew that once they launched the product positioning at a bundled price point for solution and service, they would gain share very quickly. She also talked about how the team had worked so well together, pulling all-nighters and working weekends to get the marketing kits, sales materials, PR campaign, and product positioning ready. "I can't believe we've been at this for almost six months," she concluded. "Feels like it flew by. I think we're ready."

Nolan then shared his views of Sara's accomplishments for the year, agreeing with much of her assessment. He referred to some of the metrics she had set for herself and the targets she had exceeded, those she had met well, and the one target she had missed, which she'd acknowledged. He gave his impressions of the creative skills he'd seen grow in her over the year and affirmed how she'd deliberately sought to deepen her analytical capability and how that had paid off in such a substantial way for her and for Brookreme. He then passed Sara the plate of giant white-chocolate macadamia nut cookies and she reacted with astonishment, saying, "How the hell did you remember this?"

Nolan replied sheepishly, "I didn't. I had my assistant ask your team."

Sara gave him a high five across the table.

He continued, "So what's next, Sara? As you get ready to pass the baton of the Asia work to the launch team, what are you hoping to take on next?"

"Great question. I've honestly been so buried in this work, plus all of the other routine projects for Europe and the U.S., that I really haven't given it much thought. Maybe a vacation would be good for starters!"

"It sounds like you could use one," Nolan said. "Are you planning anything?"

"Well, I was surfing some sites this morning to see what kind of deals there were," Sara replied. "I think I found a great package in Puerto Vallarta."

"Are you going to book it?"

"Well, I want to make sure things are really tied up and out the door and that my team isn't—"

Nolan interrupted her: "Book it, Sara. You need to take a break. The team will manage fine."

She held up her hand. "Got it."

"So is it hard on some level to be letting go of Asia after all the work you've put into it and the impact you've had on the success?" Nolan asked.

"Funny you should say that. I was just thinking last night that it will be weird not being part of this anymore. Like I feel so much a part of this. And I'm proud of it, you know? It was a big deal for me to uncover those trends and validate an entirely new market niche on the other side of the world. And I'm glad I stuck to my guns when some people wanted to shoot down my conclusions. I was grateful Don backed me up. That felt great. So now it's time for the baby to be born and it kind of feels like giving it up for adoption or something. I don't know if that makes any sense."

"It makes great sense, Sara. You've had a lot of ownership on this project. You've done great work. It's always hard for anyone to deal with letting go of something that's important to them. I remember Brookreme's first advertising campaign and marketing strategy. I was really proud of it. But when it came time for the sales teams to take it out to the field and the regional managers to customize it for their markets, I had to let go. It's hard."

"Yeah, that's what I'm talking about," Sara said. "Like, maybe it's just my ego or something, but what happens if they mess it up? You know?"

"Exactly," Nolan empathized. "And you know, they just might, Sara. And what's probably harder to accept is that they also just might make it even better. It's hard to imagine our hard work in the hands of others—not needing us anymore for it to be good work, isn't it?"

"Damn, Nolan, when did you get so smart?" Sara sat back in her chair with a tad bit of admiration for the boss she'd apparently long underestimated. "Maybe there's more to you than I thought!"

Nolan laughed.

At that point, there was a tap on the window. It was Nancy. Nolan motioned for her to come in. He stood in his usual gentlemanly way and shook her hand.

"Hi, Sara, good to see you," Nancy said, shaking her hand as well.

"Hey, Nancy. Good to see you too."

"Looks like you two have enjoyed a nice meal. Nolan mentioned you'd be meeting to go through your BPAP today, so I wanted to stop by and personally give you my thanks for all your work this year. It's looking like Asia is going to be a win for us this time, and I know that's in large part because of your hard work and insights. I just wanted you to know that I'm grateful."

She glanced at Nolan, who winked back at her. Clearly he'd set this up.

"Wow," Sara responded with awe. "Just how good does this get? I thought the sea bass was good, Nolan, but having the top lady make an appearance— that's over the top. Thanks, Nancy. That means a lot to me."

"My pleasure, Sara. And there's more. Nolan and I have spoken about this already. As I'm assembling the launch team in Asia, I think we've found some great local talent there to join us. As we've discovered, part of the key to success there is having local people represent us, not just the 'flying Americans.' I think in the long term they will be winners. We were able to poach a key person away from Fantronics in Shanghai. But in the near term, to be candid, I'm concerned about them getting traction. They don't know our products well, and the bundled deal has no market track record to learn from. So there's a bit of risk on the front end of this thing. How would you feel about spending six months over there to help them get the launch off the ground? I know they could use your expertise; it would give you a taste of some international experience, which couldn't hurt your career; and I know some of us back here would rest easier knowing we had a key player on the ground over there to warranty a solid entry. Jeff from finance and Lisa from HR have already signed up for the team, and San Diego will be loaning us Lana Hu from their sales team—she's been their top sales person this year. I'd want you taking the lead on the marketing implementation, but using the new team we've hired over there to get it done. What do you think?"

"Holy—" This time Sara stopped herself. She at least knew swearing at the CEO was probably not a good idea. "I guess I don't know what to say, Nancy.

Can I think about it? I mean, that's a pretty big leap. Do you think I have what it takes? I guess you wouldn't have asked if you didn't. Wow."

Nancy continued, "Well, there's no question this would be a stretch for you, and you'd be doing some new things. There would be some huge cultural shifts to make, and any new venture is going to have its bumps, so your patience would certainly get a good testing. . . ." Nancy grinned and winked at Sara, knowing that patience wasn't one of her strong suits.

Sara shot back, "Yeah, everyone knows I'm the queen of patience around here."

The three of them laughed. Nancy headed for the door. "I'll let you both get back to your conversation. Think it over, and I'll circle back with Nolan in the next couple of days. If you have any questions I can be helpful with, stop by. And again, thanks for your great work this year."

There was a pause while Sara collected herself. Even for a strong, hard-charging young woman, this was overwhelming.

"Well, Nolan, I gotta tell you, this is certainly one for the books."

"I'm sure you need some time to consider this, Sara. It's a crossroads of your career. But as I read over your personal goals for the coming year, it would seem to me that this assignment could be a great way to achieve them. You are an ambitious and talented woman, and we see your potential. I was even impressed with the metrics you included on your goals."

"Yeah, well, not all parts of the process are bad, I guess."

"Do you have some initial reservations about the opportunity?"

"Well, yeah—I mean, what if I totally flop? What if I'm just not cut out for it?"

"That could happen," Nolan calmly replied.

That was quite disarming for Sara. She'd expected him to come back with some reassuring words about how that wouldn't be the case.

He continued, "What's the worse thing that could happen if you fail?"

"I could ruin the launch?"

"Do you really think that could happen?"

"Well, maybe that's an extreme example," Sara allowed. "But I could certainly screw up pretty badly."

"Yes, you certainly could, and most likely you will. It may not be 'badly,' but you will undoubtedly make mistakes, Sara. That's part of anyone's learning curve. The question is, what will you do once you've made the mistake?"

Sara was quiet—another unusual reaction for her. Being at a loss for words was never her problem. Nolan leaned forward on the table and gently began to talk again.

"Sara, you are a very talented young woman. You work hard. You are creative. And like most talented people, you are probably as much afraid of success as you are of failure. And there's no question this assignment is going to require of you some people skills you've never needed before. You know you are impatient and you know what happens when you get impatient. You've read the comments from your teammates on your BPAP, just as I have. They think the world of you, but they don't like how sharp you can be when things don't go as you planned or as quickly as you want. In Asia, it's a different game, and you're definitely going to have to adjust. I think you can do it, but you'll have to work hard. You have to believe you can do it, and you have to want it badly enough to do that hard work. Only you can make that decision. And no harm, no foul, Sara. If you decide not to take it, I'm sure there are many great things for you to work on here, and your career can continue to be every bit as bright as it has been."

Sara was still quiet, in a contemplative way Nolan had never before seen in her. He was glad to see she was really thinking.

"Gimme a few days to think about this, OK, Nolan? I don't want to make an impulsive decision here, and that's usually what I would do. There's just too much at stake. Can I get back with you in a couple of days? I'm sure I'm going to have more questions for you."

Nolan agreed. Sara thanked him for a great lunch and conversation. At the door, she turned back and said to him, "You have definitely set a whole new standard for the BPAP. Now this is how the process oughta work!"

He laughed and simply said, "Thanks for pushing me. It was really my pleasure. I'll talk to you in a couple of days."

For the Moments Yet to Come . . .

1. What processes in your organization have become like scripts that get followed? Do you see places where standardization has created a mindlessness about how people approach their work?

2. Where does your organization struggle with process? Do you need to pay attention to some large inefficiencies that are siphoning off energy that could be directed elsewhere?

3. Do you know what your own dreams are for your organization? How do your dreams help propel your performance goals?

4. Do you know the desires of those with whom you lead regarding their futures? Do you see untapped potential in your organization that, if pushed, could yield extraordinary results?

CHAPTER FIVE

A DIAMOND IN FORMATION

The Death of Arrogance, The Dare of Generosity

The jungle is dark but full of diamonds
A diamond is rough and hard to the touch
It's dark there, but full of diamonds. . . .

Arthur Miller, *Death of a Salesman*

Opportunity: Participate and contribute generously, stop doling out advice, to engage leaders in an exploration of deep development.

Ever been up this creek without a paddle?

Sara was still reeling from her conversation with Nolan two days earlier. She'd hardly slept. She experienced alternating waves of elation and panic as she contemplated the assignment in Asia. Her excitement led her down the fantasy of one day having Nancy's job—rising from triumph to triumph to be CEO. She would return from Asia just in time for Nolan's retirement, which would make her the perfect choice to succeed him. After about five years, she could move out to a line job and run one of the geographies, and of course she'd have to turn it around, but that would pave the way for her returning to corporate as Nancy's COO. Then, a few years later, Nancy would be ready to hand Sara the reins. She could really see this happening over the course of the next dozen years. The vision was so clear, it was almost as if it *had* happened already.

After a few minutes of bliss, Sara was jolted out of her trance by worrying suspicions. What if this was just Nolan's way of getting her off his back? What if he felt so threatened by her nipping at his heels that he had carefully constructed this ploy to get her out to Asia, where she'd crash and burn? Nolan wouldn't have to fire her—her failure would take care of that. She'd have to protect herself by negotiating an ironclad deal with a golden parachute if things went wrong. Maybe Nolan wasn't even conscious of what he was doing to get rid of her. Or maybe he actually *did* believe in her and was giving her a chance. Or maybe . . .

"Urgh, this is exhausting," Sara moaned under her breath. She gathered up her files and laptop to head to the Asia team's weekly session in the former conference room 8A, which had been suitably rechristened the PacRim War Room.

After nearly six months of work, the room really looked like a war zone. It was covered in flip chart pages several deep. Posters of Shanghai, Hong Kong, Singapore, and Malaysia were on the walls, with menus from their local favorite Thai takeout place, a Chinese calendar, and "Brookreme" written out in chopsticks taped together above the whiteboard. The garbage cans were full of empty water bottles, Diet Coke cans, and white takeout boxes. KIT KAT had become the team's candy of choice, and there were three cases of them on the book shelf from the local wholesale warehouse. Among many reasons for this candy of choice was its ironic slogan: "a simple, uncomplicated chocolate candy that lets you live on the light side of life. It has light, crispy wafers in chocolate that complement your lighthearted, positive approach to life." Living on the light side of life was something Brookreme people only dreamed about, and they all knew it. Several empty KIT KAT boxes were now holding pencils, pens, whiteboard markers, and note pads. The long hours of arguments and strategizing were almost audible even when the room was empty.

Sara hated to be late, so she always tried to get to these sessions early. She was usually the first to complain and take jabs at anyone who arrived late. Today, though she was not last, she was later than usual.

"Ooohhh, she's slippin'," joked Lisa from HR. Sara privately wondered if Lisa or Jeff knew she was being asked to join them on the launch team.

"Hey, can't be the pacesetter every time, now can I?" Sara jabbed right back.

"So how'd your BPAP go?" Jeff asked. It seemed an innocent question; Sara had let them all know in her usual colorful way that it had been approaching.

"Actually, it went pretty well," Sara answered with a tone of pleasant surprise in her voice.

"Shoot, from you that's a real rave," another team member lobbed in.

Everyone laughed, including Sara, as she scratched her nose with a certain finger clearly in the direction of her jesting teammate. Not certain how politically wise it would be to let them know of the offer on the table, she had concluded it would probably be best not to bring it up. Of course, inside she was dying to gloat about how Nancy had made her cameo appearance at the session to make the offer personally, and how Nolan had had a gourmet catered lunch brought in for the conversation. But she didn't want to burn all that political capital with people she might have to work with and rely on for the next couple of years.

Today's agenda item was finalizing the first-hundred-days plan. They were at T minus fifty-eight days away from opening the office in Shanghai. Activity had reached a feverish pitch. The broad entry strategy was baked and the marketing and sales blitz was ready to roll. They'd been through two passes on the detailed first-hundred-days plan. Elliot was now joining the meetings by video conference from Australia, because his people were going to be heavily involved in getting operations up and running.

Elliot had done a great job helping to build the team and rally his Sydney people around this strategy, but what Sara really wanted to know was whether he had any say in her offer. The two of them had not hit it off too well when they first met about a year earlier. Sara had flown to Sydney to help them roll out their bundled solutions offerings, and though she had been greatly appreciated by her peers in Sydney, she had felt that Elliot treated her like some executive assistant who had been mistakenly promoted to a "real" job. She'd found him condescending and disrespectful. During the training session she conducted, he had chimed in every ten or fifteen minutes and basically repeated what she'd just said. Afterward, he'd told her, "I was just trying to help you bridge the cultural differences. Some people here just don't speak 'American,' so I thought I'd just help you out." She'd said to him, "Next time, wait till I ask for help before you give it." Since then, any time they'd been in a meeting together, including the Asia meetings, things were cordial on the surface, with a clear undercurrent of rivalry, at least to Sara. Elliot was so aloof it was hard for her to guess just what he was actually thinking.

Elliot finally logged onto the video conference. The team always had fun imitating the delayed motions and lip movements of Elliot's conference appearances, complete with his Kiwi accent. Crocodile Dundee always seemed to make channeled appearances through several of the team members.

Elliot's signature "Hello friends!" greeting came over the mic. The chorus of greetings from the war room team was typically warm and fun.

He continued, "Did you all have a chance to read over the latest version of the first-hundred-days plan I emailed yesterday? I'd like to start by going over some of the leftover questions from last week's session to see if we can lock down at least eight weeks, so we can make sure by the end of next week everyone on the ground in Asia knows exactly who's doing what and when. Sound good?"

"Rock on," "Go for it," and "Sounds like a plan" came from a number of those in the war room. Sara could feel her impatience already mounting, knowing how tedious this conversation was going to get. Her mind was still on the decision she needed to make; though she was clearly leaning toward accepting, she remained uneasy about it.

"Sara, did you have a chance to confirm whether or not we can get the folks from the American embassy, that Chinese pop star, and the Shanghai Business and Economic Bureau at the reception that first weekend?" Elliot calmly asked.

Sara was jarred from her daydreaming. She'd heard the question. She couldn't believe she'd dropped the ball. Everyone was staring at her, waiting for her answer. The silence was a bit longer than Sara ever usually waited to reply, and around the table a couple of brows furrowed ever so slightly.

"Sara?" Elliot prompted.

With as much finesse as she could muster, Sara opened her files, appearing to scan down her notes, trying to look ever so politely skeptical. Then she said, "Gosh, Elliot, you know, somehow I had in my notes that deliverable being due next week. I still have calls out to folks over there, but I haven't firmed it up because, to be honest, I've been buried in other things and, again, had in my notes it was to be done for next week."

"I remember that, too, Elliot," said Lisa, riding to Sara's rescue. Sara was boiling inside from embarrassment and doing everything she could not to show it.

"I have it right here in the minutes that you'd have it firmed up by today's date," Elliot said.

Another teammate in the war room winced toward Sara and said, "I'm afraid that's what the minutes do say, Sara."

Why this was such a big deal was beyond Sara. There was still plenty of time to get the event planned and the right people there. So she tried to brush it off, saying, "Well, sorry then, I'll make sure I have it firmed up for next week."

She assumed it was over. But it wasn't. Elliot let out a large sigh, shaking his head slowly as though the disappointment were too much to bear. "You know, mates, when you folks in Chicago drop the ball like this, it just makes more work for us. You have way more resources than we do. It just doesn't make sense why things like this have to fall through the cracks. Thanks anyway, Sara, but I'll just go ahead and have my folks finalize it from here."

The tension in the room could be cut with a knife. Sara was biting her lip hard. Al, being the consummate middle man, tried to mediate the tense moment. "Elliot, can you help us understand why having it by next week is a problem? Sara's already got things in the works and she's already reached out to some people in Asia. Don't we risk confusing them if they have to deal with someone different now?"

Elliot pounced. "The problem is that my people here have a lot of things to coordinate for that opening weekend. And everything hinges on who's going to be at that reception. We're hoping to make a lot of connections that evening and the guest list is critical to the kinds of sales calls we can set up afterwards. We've talked about this to death. Relationships in Asia are critical. They are everything. If my people have to wait another week, who knows what we may lose?"

Al thought Elliot was being unusually melodramatic, but he didn't want to make any more waves. "I see your point, Elliot. I guess that makes sense," he said without sounding all that convinced.

Elliot continued, "Sara, if you could simply forward me all the contact information you have, who you've talked to, and who you are waiting for, that would be helpful. And please try and make sure you read the minutes after these meetings from now on, OK? We all know you are very busy, but so are we. Maybe if you had your assistant go through the minutes and highlight key deliverables of yours and have her put them in your calendar, it might help you remember better."

That was clearly uncalled for. The war room team was shocked and pissed off at Elliot's uncouth arrogance.

Jeff tried to score a point on the board. "You know, Elliot, we are all busy and tired. Every one of us has too many balls in the air, and not one of us has hit every deadline perfectly. We're under a lot of pressure here too, and it doesn't help to make comments like that at this hour of the game."

Sara, seething, wished she had simply lied. She should have told Elliot the guest list was completely firmed up and that she'd email it to him the next day. Then she could have just finished it and no one would have known the difference.

"What do you mean, 'comments like that,' Jeff?" Elliot's voice was a bit miffed. "All I was doing was being candid with my colleague. Just trying to offer her a bit of coaching to help her, that's all. Really, Jeff, no need to get defensive."

Sara was now gripping the table hard. She knew her control was ebbing away fast, and the others could feel it too.

Jeff started to reply, "Elliot, I'm *not* getting defensive, I'm simply pointing out that—" but Sara cut him off.

"Elliot, I don't know where you come off trying to offer me your lousy advice over the TV. I didn't ask for it. You have a nasty habit of giving people advice they don't ask for. I don't want your people's help. And it will take me twice as much time to compile everything to help your people start from scratch as it would take for me to simply finish it. I'll have the data for the event done by the end of the week and I'll email it as soon as it's final. Don't have them call anyone I've spoken to. Al's right, you'll just make it worse for us. And knowing some of your people, they'd probably screw it up anyway. I'm sick and tired of cleaning up their messes. Last time your teenage prodigy PR person sent press releases all over the Pacific Rim, it took me a week to get them all retracted because they were full of wrong information. They have plenty of their own work to do; I don't want them messing with my stuff. It's bad enough I'm going to have to spend the next year baby-sitting them over there, following them around mopping up. Let's at least try and get off to a decent start with the people in this market before we send them running to the competition. Now I'd suggest we move on to the next agenda item, Elliot."

The room was icy and quiet. Sara couldn't believe she'd just let fly what she did. She knew the minute she finished that she just might have sabotaged the opportunity she'd been offered. She knew Elliot would be on the phone to Nancy within the hour. She fought back tears.

The team around the table was very uncomfortable. Al looked at the screen and said quietly, "Let's take a quick ten before we move on, Elliot."

Several teammates knew Sara was shaken and upset. They came over behind her and rubbed her back. Lisa bent down and gave her a hug, saying softly, "Don't sweat it, kiddo. He asked for it."

Sara walked over to get a bottle of water, clearly distraught. Jeff followed, put his hand on her shoulder, and eagerly asked, "Hey, does that mean you'll be coming on the team? That would be awesome!"

Sara finished her chug of water and looked at Jeff. "Thanks, Jeff. I appreciate that. But after that little episode, who knows what's going to happen? I just may have landed myself a luxurious tour of duty in the mail room."

For the Moment

How do you respond to advice like Elliot's?
How do people respond when you give advice like that?
How do you feel about Sara's response to Elliot?
What would you tell her if you were her boss?

If you work in an organization, you can't escape the inevitable experience of your own failure. And you don't get to escape the failure of others, either. So what to do with failure? Everyone knows that leaders come with flaws that reveal themselves in sometimes unpredictable, often detrimental ways. And in the last decade, a major cottage industry has sprung up in the area of executive coaching to help manage the plethora of leadership issues facing the managerial ranks of organizations. I think there is enormous value in leaders seeking advice from objective outsiders on issues of their own development and the charters of their roles. What has troubled me is that the executive coaching concept has grown beyond its original intent of offering genuinely caring advice to an "I'm here to fix you" approach, and the way in which this tends to happen is frequently problematic. As Steven Berglas says in his perceptive *Harvard Business Review* article, "The Very Real Dangers of Executive Coaching":

The popularity of executive coaching owes much to the modern craze for easy answers . . . To achieve fast results, many popular executive coaches model their interventions after those used by sports coaches, employing techniques that reject out of hand any introspective process that can take time and cause "paralysis by analysis." The idea that an executive coach can improve performance quickly is a great selling point to CEOs, who put the bottom line first. Yet that approach tends to gloss over any unconscious conflict the employee may have. This can have disastrous consequences for the company in the long term and can exacerbate the psychological damage to the person targeted for help.

> *Eagles may soar high, but weasels don't get sucked into*
> *jet engines.*
> DAVID BRENT, *regional manager* WERNHAM HOGG
> *The Office*

THE FALLACY OF "COACHING": DON'T MAKE PEOPLE YOUR PROJECTS

When entering the realm of helping others pursue personal change, one must strike a dangerously delicate balance. There are boundaries easily breeched, to the detriment of those we want to help. The outcome is harm, not help. How do we build commitment in others to pursue their own growth? How do we help them hear how others experience them, especially when that experience may be outside of their intentions?

When I work with my clients and with those who report to me in my organization, I work hard (not always successfully) to get clear on what their aspirations are for growth as leaders and professionals. I will candidly, and caringly, share with them how I experience them and how I observe others to experience them. And I will share my thoughts on what the potential unintended consequences of their actions could be. Then I will invite them into conversations that explore alternative choices for behaviors that might get them closer to the outcomes or influence they want. I deliberately avoid ever indicating that my suggestions or perceptions are *right* or that what I am offering is a *prescription* for change. We are simply exploring together the implications of behaviors that appear to be unproductive or unhelpful. In a reporting relationship, sometimes I need to make clear the performance consequences of such choices, and on rare occasion I need to be clear about the potential hazards if the unintended consequences or shortfalls don't change. My hope is to have people aspire to greater levels of their own capability, not to paralyze them with feelings of inadequacy as though their shortcomings and failures will spell doom for their futures. I've seen too many unfortunate examples of leaders who punitively berate those they lead with harsh, judgmental messages of incompetence. It pains me to see leaders' spirits wilt and their perseverance wane when confidence has been withdrawn from them.

Today, most organizations have some type of multirater feedback system. Data are collected about an individual leader from their boss, their peers, their direct reports, and occasionally customers or suppliers. Often referred to as *360-degree feedback* or simply *a 360,* the process of multirater feedback was intended to instigate a broader, richer conversation about how people were experienced in complex environments in which they interacted with many people. It was intended to remove some of the extreme subjectivity in performance conversations in which leaders would offer evaluations of others with little direct data. It is a great concept when used as a means to an end. Unfortunately, in many organizations the collection of data has become the end. A leader will gather a set of people who contributed to the report into a conference room, read the summary conclusions out loud to them, and ask if there are any questions (of course there won't be any). This allows that leader to check off his "I processed my 360" box.

The process of collecting multirater data should never be more than a good excuse to have a rich conversation with others by providing them a safe mechanism to offer candid views. It's the *conversation* about the data and its meaning that strengthens a leader's ability to effectively adjust her behavior. The feedback that's been gathered, in and of itself, is useless. But in many organizations, it has become less about the conversation and more of a weapon. In fact, in one client organization, the only time a 360 was done on someone was when they were in trouble and the organization was mounting a case to fire them. If you were asked to participate in evaluating someone as a rater, you knew that you held that person's future in the palm of your hand. This makes a lot of people uncomfortable.

What's unfortunate is the lost opportunity. It takes courage for a leader to invite such data, especially data that might be hard to hear. And it takes courage for leaders to offer such data, especially in the face of political risks. The latent power resident in the data for positive change and enhanced relationships is lost because the bridge it was intended to build between leaders winds up creating a greater gulf. I've seen leaders read their data reports and say things like, "I know who said that. He's still mad because I didn't assign him to the project he requested last year and he never got over it," or, "Well, we've just been through a lot of change. I'm not surprised they are all this upset," or, "Wow, all 4's and 5's—I must be doing something right." These are predictable reactions in organizations in which *conversation* about the data isn't the goal—*collecting* it is.

Let's be clear. Collecting data in the service of fixing people—or, worse, punishing people—is arrogant and destructive. This is one case in which *no process* would in fact be better than a *bad process*.

As I stated earlier in this book, most emerging leaders come wired with a strong fear of failure, counterbalanced by an unusually high level of passion. Ben, the ink still wet on his M.B.A. diploma, offered this testimony of his anxiety: "I am worried about letting people down . . . I am worried about having a lot of excitement and passion, but then not knowing what to do next. I am worried that I am impulsive and emotional and that I lack real wisdom and leadership. I am worried that I lack real training. I wonder if I am truly dynamic enough that people will follow me." Though ingrained with an exhaustive fear of failure, their determination hasn't been quelled. Ben followed this list by saying, "I'm still excited about my vision, and I can't wait to live into the actualization of it." Sadly, this excitement is often experienced as brashness and impulsivity by many incumbent leaders, and it is easily critiqued and dismissed.

This is dangerous territory, as the next generation of leaders is particularly sensitive to the criticism of others, especially when it comes outside the relative safety of genuine relationship. They typically view processes such as multirater feedback devices as managerial ploys, not as honest attempts at meaningful conversation. Kip, a rising star at his technology firm, said it this way: "I desire transparency and the freedom to fail." In contrast, the incumbent leaders charged with developing these leaders have themselves rarely had meaningful conversation about their own development.

As leaders they are more accustomed to an occasional cryptic comment by a boss intended to convey some dissatisfaction with something. As such, both incumbent and emerging leaders begin the process of exploring personal growth with varying degrees of discomfort and anxiety. But if the next generation of leaders is going to be well prepared to lead in contexts of greater uncertainty and opportunity, both incumbent and emerging leaders are going to have to step up to the plate.

THE GENERATIVE LEADER: THE GIFT THAT KEEPS ON GIVING

It's impressive to see a seasoned executive with a stellar career continue to reinvent their leadership, and adapt to their context by taking on personal shortcomings in the service of their organization.

One CEO I spoke with (let's call him Peter)—an enormously humble man who preferred to remain anonymous and would be the first to tell you that his successful run as CEO was far from just his doing—is a great example. He would also be the first to admit that some of his own leadership behaviors had to change continuously to enable him to contribute effectively to the leadership formation of others. Listen to his reflections on his leadership:

"I know how much damage I have done and caused people to underperform because of my unfair or inappropriate criticism and anger. Earlier in my career, it wasn't easy for me to trust people. People were chased away and shut down. Some people never recover from the damage done by harsh leaders."

At that point in my conversation with him, he looked down and I could see his eyes welling up. I was amazed at the level of introspection this man engaged in. We explored a number of the relationships he'd formed with leaders around him. The story of his relationship with Phil, his then-CFO—a relationship Peter had maintained through several job transitions over more than ten years—offered a very interesting look at the impact Peter had had on leaders in the organization. Peter said of Phil:

"Early on, because I was being so hard on him, it was hindering his performance. I was unnaturally limiting his ability. He had so many things cluttering his mind when he spoke with me that he couldn't think clearly. I didn't recognize that at the time, but as he developed and became more confident in his environment, it was easier for him to push back, which is what I wanted him to do. He started building his knowledge and comfort, and as he did so my confidence in him grew, as did his own self-confidence."

I also had the opportunity to speak with Phil. Here's what he told me about Peter's leadership transformation over the years:

> When I first met Pete, I got started, as we all did, in "Pete boot camp." In those days, there was no such thing as being a mentor. You were expected to be fully equipped to take over a job instantaneously. Whether or not you had the background was irrelevant. He wasn't patient. If you made a mistake, it would be met with a glower or harsh admonition. One day, I did something that displeased him, and he hunted me down and berated me in such a way that it really annoyed me. I confronted him on his behavior and said I was going to leave. That event led Pete to think maybe he hadn't given me enough of a shot. So now I have a little bit more of a grace period because he's figured out he should have mentored me from the beginning. Then things started to get better. One day Pete said, "Do you think my guys respect me?" And I said, "No. I think they are afraid to death of you. If you want to be a leader who leads by fear, it might work for some, but it isn't working for you."
>
> Pete took that little comment and began the process of reinventing himself. He worked very hard not to be so intimidating, to listen more, to be more gracious. From then on, I had the opportunity to give him all kinds of advice about his behavior—most wouldn't have the courage to do it—and he listened very closely. Now we have the kind of relationship where I tell him things nobody else would. One day after a major speech to the street, media, and board, I said, "I don't want to talk about how good you were because you know you were good. I want to tell you how proud I am of who you've become—what an incredible human being you have become."
>
> Pete is an amazing man and leader. He's probably reinvented himself at least three times since I've known him. Would I put my life in his hands and trust him with it? Yes I would. That's saying something. There are times when he aggravates me like he can't believe. I knew he was taking a risk on me, and most companies are looking to get us geezers out the door, and yet he trusted me enough that I could fit into this role and be successful.

Pete was overwhelmed when he was made CEO. He is as humble a man as they come. Today his stock is selling at top dollar, his board loves him, he's as disciplined as they come, and he lives as modestly as any CEO I've ever known—and I've worked for Welch, Bradshaw, some top operating guys. Pete has distinguished himself as an excellent operating leader. He doesn't have the need for the great trappings of life. He and his wife have now jointly decided to go and do something very different, and help those less fortunate than they are.

After years, and an envious run as CEO by any standards, Peter and his wife decided to retire early to pursue charitable faith-based work together. Many of the analysts on Wall Street who'd come to admire and respect his work as CEO also hailed him as a leader for taking this next step in his life.

Hearing the impact Peter had on others, like Phil, isn't the best part of the story. How Peter transmitted the DNA of caring for and developing leaders throughout the organization is really what makes this a generative story, and Peter a generative leader. Listen to how Peter talks about the process of finding and developing leaders:

When you get out into the organization and really listen to what people are doing, you realize there are all kinds of people with ideas about change, enthusiasm, and energy, [who are] doing great things. There isn't a shortage of them. There's *lots* of talent. But it needs to be developed. The best way to develop it is to move it around. I am fortunate that I have many companies throughout the organization that I can move people around in. In our executive team meetings we are constantly talking about leadership development, [which] people are ready to move, and what we are doing to get others ready. I wanted visibility into the organization's pipeline of leaders. We created processes that allowed me to have visibility to see other folks down in the organization. At first it wasn't a conscious way to find leaders, it just happened. It was originally meant to accelerate change in the organization. In doing so, we made it possible for people who were willing to step up and make a difference to show us who they were. It expanded the audience with whom I normally met. More than just say hello, but hear what they were doing, see their creativity, dedication, and enthusiasm. And to make sure we had quality conversations, I knew I had to be in their world, not have them come to mine. I wasn't trying to "go around" the hierarchy. I found that the normal business review process is ineffective at creative places for conversation. It might tell you someone is a good presenter, but you don't get to meet people and understand what they are capable of. It can be a negative experience sometimes.

Whenever we had major training, I would go to the classes all over the world—between four and six a year. I'd go there to thank people for being willing to learn more for the good of the company. I would go around and ask people why they'd volunteer for the training, what they'd hoped for. I'd ask specific questions about how the change process was working in their part of the organization. By going to all those classes it established a link between me and those being trained. So when I went back to those business units, those leaders who'd been trained were there to display some of their projects. When I got into the details of their initiatives, I could clearly see people who were committed, enthusiastic, working hard, and making progress. I realized that there are people at all levels of the company doing very interesting work, committed to making a difference, and actually making great change, often in spite of management. The issue wasn't that we didn't have people; the issue was we didn't know who they were, and we didn't have a mechanism for making sure they were being moved around into assignments earlier in their careers. So we greatly strengthened the management development process all throughout the organization.

One of the many leaders whose career was dramatically impacted by Peter's personal investment was Nate. Peter realized that moving people around in the organization is a vital part of building capable leaders, but often very difficult to do. It requires levels of commitment and sacrifice not everyone is willing to give. He says, "I couldn't get people to do some of the things we needed them to do—especially taking on new jobs—without the relationship in place to ask them. My confidence in people, and the relationship I establish with them, makes a huge difference in getting people to take on bigger and harder jobs." Nate had been very successful building sales processes in one part of the organization, and Peter was eager for him to move into broader assignments to expand his success. But Nate was reluctant. Here's how Nate describes his ascent into leading what is now one of the primary business units of the organization:

Pete took time to talk with me and question me about how I saw running my business, and how we could help the company on principles we both shared. About five years ago he contacted me and told me I had a bright future at the company. He saw something in me that could be developed. He started encouraging me to take on bigger roles. I'm not the kind of person to jump into big jobs easily. At first, I said no because I didn't feel I was ready. He felt I was ready, but accepted my answer. I said no again a year later, and then finally I said yes six months later, a year and a half after he first approached me. To be honest, my self-confidence was not strong. Another reason for my reluctance, frankly, was the fact that I feared having to sell my soul. As a management company president, you really have to commit to the organization—deal with the analysts and external constituents. It's a huge commitment and I wasn't sure I was ready. A combination of things changed by the third time he asked. First, I would never know if I could do it or not if I didn't try. I thought it might be the last time I was asked and I might have regretted later not trying. I still feared failing and not liking the job. Pete was flabbergasted that I said yes. He shared his personal experience of leaving his home to take the COO job at headquarters, and how it strengthened his relationship with his wife because of the crucible of the move. Hearing about his personal experiences really helped me think about the decision.

Pete is very prepared to talk about deep issues in his life, and about life issues that make leadership hard. That's a side of him I don't think many people see. Some saw him as occasionally abrupt and not particularly sensitive. He talked about his learning curve to not be judgmental, to listen more, and to encourage others. It was clear he was developing his own leadership quite a *lot*. He shed tears in the forums before he left, and when you saw that side of him, it was quite positive because you saw the depth of his character and humanity.

Now that I'm into the job a year and a half, I see he was right. I do have things to offer. Whatever he saw in me that I didn't see in myself is now more evident to the organization, and to me. I'm reveling in the fact that I am enjoying this job that I thought I wouldn't. I'm enjoying "relaxing" into leadership. It's a complex business, having to talk to analysts on the fly. I wasn't as prepared as I like to be. I've "learned to play" with the organization—my skepticism, as a non-American man, about typical corporate America, has changed. I see that at the top levels of organizations there are many positive experiences that allow me to be part of the organization in a good way. There is a positive social aspect of what we can do as an organization. When you think about how much we did for the [December 2004] tsunami disaster, for example, you get a sense of a larger purpose that does good for the world that is unique to this level of an organization. We reward people who do great things in the community. I might have thought it was just corporate spin at one point, but now I see the tremendous good we do for the world.

I recognize myself now coming alongside others and seeing in them my own "schoolboy nervousness" that can come from inter-acting with senior leaders. What I have learned in the last eighteen months is exponential to what I've learned in the last five years—as a leader, as a person. I'm very fortunate to have had this experi-ence. I'm now mentoring others in the community, and some that I've mentored can see how I am personally changing. The ethical standards that Pete sets, which were already quite strong, raised the bar for everyone in the organization. It's something we don't even think about—it's just understood—the standard is the highest it can be. People want to come and work for us because we're known that way. Pete's humility is quite overpowering. He believes leader-ship resides in many different facets—personal and professional. What he did with our leadership program set a standard for leader-ship work as a real corporate process for developing leaders to which most organizations never aspire.

Nate had these words of advice to offer incumbent leaders seeking to develop the next generation of leaders around them:

If you have a vision for someone's ability, even in the face of their own protestations, you should stick with them. Pete didn't give up on me, and didn't let my reluctance get in the way of his faith in me. He waited and kept working with me, and kept coming back to me. That says a lot about someone who is prepared to stay with someone. I think seeing a person's blemishes and quirkiness as potential assets is a great thing for leaders. Individuality is a beauti-ful thing. I'm part of a team, but I think we need to start looking at the differences in others rather than simply looking at the "scripts" and concluding that someone is "off script and doesn't fit." I don't get the sense that corporate America is all that comfortable with valuing those who are "off script." Perhaps it's time to throw the scripts away. Had Pete not been willing to suspend judgment with me, I would not be in this job today. He was willing to see underneath my own apprehension the unique things I could bring to the organization that I wasn't yet capable of seeing. That's the mark of a great leader—to see in others what they can't yet see for themselves.

Of the many stunning things in this story, what clearly stands out is that the development of leadership is generative. Peter was every bit as in the process of becoming a leader as he was in engaging others in the process of their own becoming, and he let them see it. He participated in and contributed to their development, and he invited them into his own. He didn't see himself as the sage dispenser of wisdom. He saw himself as much on a journey as they were.

For the Moment

Can you describe a time when you've reinvented yourself?

Have you ever worked with someone like Peter?

Would you describe your leadership style as generative? Would others?

What will be your legacy with regard to leadership development?

DIAMOND MINING: THE ART OF LEADERSHIP FORMATION

The Corporate Executive Board of the Corporate Leadership Council did an in-depth study assessing the potential of rising talent within an organization. Some of their findings are quite sobering:

- Ninety-seven percent of organizations report significant leadership gaps, with more than 40 percent of survey respondents deeming leadership deficiencies "acute."
- Seventy-four percent of organizations report that leadership gaps have a "modest" or "significant" negative impact on product innovation, talent retention, financial performance, and customer relationships.

- Fifty-nine percent of organizations report that failure of externally hired executives is a "significant problem," and 50 percent report that failure of internally promoted leaders is a "significant problem."
- Of these high-potential failures, 51 percent result from lower than anticipated ability, aspiration, or engagement, and 21 percent are company-induced stalls.

These statistics are staggering when the implications are considered. If just over half of those emerging leaders we deem as "the future" are flaming out because they aren't as good as anyone thought, don't have the apparent desire to grow, and aren't being engaged by the organization to the degree needed, what does that say about what people believe that the process of developing leaders actually requires? It would appear that organizations often grossly underestimate the requirements of securing a cadre of well-prepared leaders for the future.

One of my all-time favorite books is *The Art of Possibility* by Rosamund Stone Zander and Benjamin Zander. Ben is a world-renowned conductor of the Boston Philharmonic and teaches at the New England Conservatory in Boston. In the book, he writes about the natural performance anxieties with which his students arrive at the conservatory. He describes the academically heretical practice of telling everyone on the first day of class that they will all get an A at the end of the semester. Then they each must write him a letter that first week, as though it were the end of the semester, and describe to him what they did to earn the A. He says the process transforms the way in which people approach learning and personal expression. It completely changes the game of "becoming." Listen to how he describes it:

> The practice of giving the A both invents and recognizes a universal desire in people to contribute to others, no matter how many barriers there are to its expression. We can choose to validate the apathy of a boss, a player, or a student and become resigned ourselves, or we can choose to honor in them an unfulfilled yearning to make a difference . . . Unlike success or failure, contribution has no other side. It is not arrived at by comparison. All at once I found that the fearful question, "Is it enough?" and the even more fearful

question, "Am I loved for who I am, or for what I have accomplished?" could both be replaced by the joyful question, "How will I be a contribution today?" . . . Naming oneself and others as a contribution produces a shift away from self-concern and engages us in a relationship with others that is an arena for making a difference.

QUADNOCULAR VISION AS THE KEY TO GENEROUS CONTRIBUTION OF MINING DIAMONDS

Participating with and contributing generously to others to invite deeper development requires a unique ability to hold multiple perspectives at one time. To illustrate the need, I use this image with my clients. It is an image of a diamond forming in coal thousands of feet below the earth's surface under multiple tons of pressure and heat. What I say to them is that there are really four images here, not just one. Two will be  obvious: the coal and the unformed gem. Two will not be obvious but are every bit as important. One came before the obvious pair: the set of diamonds that were previously extracted from this coal. The fourth comes after the others: the stone as it *will be* when fully formed and polished. A gifted leader will be able to see all four, here and within those with whom she leads. Here is a detailed description of these four images:

1. *The coal.* The hard, crusty, pressure-packed material that works against the stone to build its strength and beauty. It must be carefully dug away to liberate the stone from its habitat when it is ready. Most people either overly attend to their coal or deny having any at all. Leaders who pay excessive attention to the coal induce feelings of inadequacy and fear. Leaders who ignore the coal run the risk of liberating narcissists or setting people up for detrimental failure.

2. *The diamond in its current form.* The process of becoming can be relished and enjoyed if we look at every aspect of a forming asset in real time, as it is. Even in its unformed, unpolished, not-

yet-fully-valuable state, there is beauty in this gem. We must remain focused on the process of excavation by holding in view the coal, as well as the new appearances of the gem at every step.

3. *The polished diamonds that have already been unearthed.* Though not in this image, there are beautifully polished gems that have already been extracted from the mine and are on display, being enjoyed and contributing. Similarly, it is important to hold in view the existing gifts people come equipped with. Too often, organizations ask their leaders to deny the talents with which they came, rendering their past experiences and accomplishments inconsequential. Instead of celebrating these as part of the reason they were invited in the first place, organizations often choose to be threatened by the towering strengths leaders sport.

4. *The diamond as it will be when it is polished.* It is terrifying to acknowledge one's own greatness as it becomes great. As Ben, the young M.B.A., described earlier, the fear-based questions of adequacy and sufficiency get in the way of enjoying this state. I find it is essential to help leaders in the process of excavation to keep a keen eye on the gem, imagining it as it will be when it is fully excavated and polished. This beautifully accelerates the development process.

Holding all four of these perspectives in view *at the same time* is the true art of helping leaders become. And it requires a level of participation of both leaders engaged in the journey of leadership formation. Overfocusing on any one aspect of the picture, at the expense of other aspects, risks hampering the process of formation. Worse, it risks stalling it. Balancing them all invites the burgeoning of amazing talent.

> The word "generosity" includes the term "gen" which we also find in the words "gender," "generation," and "generativity." This term, from the Latin genus and the Greek genos, refers to our being of one kind. Generosity is a giving that comes from the knowledge of that intimate bond. . . . Generosity creates the family it believes in.
>
> HENRI NOUWEN
> *Return of the Prodigal Son*

THE BRIDGE TO RELATIONSHIP: GENEROUSLY PARTICIPATE IN DIAMOND MINING TO ENGAGE LEADERS IN EXCAVATING LEADERSHIP GREATNESS

Volumes have been written on the topic of developing others. Dispensing advice is a well-honed skill that most have cultivated to excess. The problem with advice, of course, is that it tends to extract the advisor from the process of formation. A veritable sideliner, all he must do is dispense advice and go. As the Polish writer Stanislaw Lec once said, "You will always find some Eskimos ready to instruct the Congolese on how to cope with heat waves." Contribution, by contrast, is a messier process requiring skin in the game from both leaders, *both* acknowledging their own formation. Your own experience has undoubtedly distinguished this for you. Add those priceless lessons to this starter list of ideas about how to make your own contribution.

1. *Shed entitlement.* One of the most painful aspects of the corporate world—and frankly, it's one I see a great deal in emerging leaders—is a sense of entitlement. Approaching the process of making or receiving contribution with "this is due me" or "you're lucky I'm here" is not only distasteful, it limits access to deeper opportunities for personal change. Entitlement is a fungus typically bred in environments of insufficient feedback devices, unhealthy levels of competition, and excessive nurturing of prima donnas. It spreads self-involvement that prohibits leaders from expressing their natural desire to contribute to others.

2. *Don't feel small in the presence of other's diamonds.* Some people have a really hard time enjoying, much less acknowledging, the beauty in others—their gifts, their ideas, their accomplishments. It's tragic. Instead, their own conditioning has prepared them to compare and to perceive themselves, or others, falling short. They choose to feel small in comparison. The contempt shown to leaders because they are gifted is a destructive element in environments where zero-sum thinking prevails. "The more affirmation you get for your talent, the less there will be for me" underlies some

leaders' thinking. Abandon such thinking and learn to revel in the success of others. You will learn to enjoy your own gifts even more as you learn to enjoy the gifts of others.

3. *Acknowledge your own coal.* Never begin the process of entering the formation of another leader without demonstrating awareness of your own shortfalls. Use your own experiences, especially the mistakes you've made with your coal, as a way to contribute to the development of others. Your credibility as a fellow sojourner in the process of leadership formation will be greatly enhanced if you can let others see how your coal is transformed into priceless gifts.

4. *Don't leave leadership formation to chance.* Although I talked about the hollow processes of leadership development to which organizations often default, I am by no means advocating for no process at all. Invest heavily in robust processes that honor and encourage the deep work of leadership formation. Don't wait until your organization really is shorthanded for key leadership assignments. Build pipelines of rich experiences, assessment, accountability, and celebration that enable leaders to become at every stage of their career and in every assignment for which they are given a chance. And by all means, if you have processes that aren't yielding necessary results, don't keep them in place just because they've always been there or because you don't want to hurt the feelings of those running them. Redesign them, or dismantle them and begin again.

5. *Seek to be known as generous.* Since you are building a reputation of some kind anyway, you might as well build one that gets you known for giving. Make deliberate contributions of your time, experience, affirmation, painful lessons, and successes to those leaders around you and their journeys of becoming. When others leave your presence, work to ensure that their conclusion about their time with you is "That was helpful and valuable. I'm glad I came." Act in ways that set the example for others, raising the generative bar that entices others to give in turn.

6. *Avoid giving unsolicited advice.* For leaders, restraining the impulse to correct can be excruciating, especially when others are at risk of costly failure. Sometimes it is our job to step in and offer perspective, whether solicited or not. But in areas with the potential

for personal transformation, where quantum leaps in leadership formation can be made, it's best to offer participation first, then contribution once invited. Jumping in all at once may scare the leader back into her shell, overwhelmed and anxious about her own growth. Dropping hints to soften the blow only makes things worse. Be authentically caring about your desire to help, knowing that the recipient is not always ready to receive help when you recognize the need.

Now let's get back to Brookreme. When we left, Sara had just angrily erupted all over Elliot in response to some fairly antagonistic behavior and unsolicited, obnoxious advice. Still, her behavior wasn't helpful in an already charged environment of stress and fatigue. As she predicted, Elliot called Nancy right after the meeting.

That night, Sara got a voice mail from Nancy: "Hey, Sara, I just got off the phone with Elliot. I heard his version of what happened in today's Asia team meeting. I'd like to get your perspective. Can we meet for breakfast tomorrow morning at 7:30? I'll have food brought in. I'm copying Nolan on this voice mail too, so he knows we'll be talking. Nolan, I'll follow up with you tomorrow as well. Thanks."

Not surprisingly, Sara didn't sleep much that night. She hated it when her temper got the best of her. Try as she might, she just didn't seem able to hold her tongue when people pushed her buttons. Elliot was the worst kind of button-pusher for her. People she perceived to be condescending and dismissive always set her off, and she was even more prone to react when the offender was a man. She'd become resigned to the expectation that Nancy was going to withdraw the offer to go to Asia; if she was lucky she would at least get to keep her current job. She was gearing up to produce a credible apology; she gritted her teeth, imagining the prospect of apologizing to Elliot. She rehearsed this speech more than a dozen times in her mind during the night: what she would say to Nancy, what she imagined Nancy saying to her, what defense she would offer, how much she would blame Elliot, how much responsibility she would take. The list went on and on. It was an endless churn of words in her mind, all mixed with regret and self-defeat, with a healthy helping of self-righteousness on top.

Sara arrived at Nancy's office just before 7:30, having been at her desk since 6:00. It was unlike Sara to feel this visibly anxious about anything, but she feared this time she'd stepped way over a line from which she might not be able to recover. She lightly knocked on the window of Nancy's open door and entered to find Nancy sitting at her desk working on her laptop. Without looking up, Nancy said, "Hey, Sara, c'mon in and have a seat; I just need to finish up this email. Help yourself to coffee and whatever else they brought in for us." On the rolling catering cart there were bagels, muffins, fresh fruit and yogurt, a pitcher of orange juice, and two Thermoses of coffee, with mugs, plates, and all of the appropriate coffee condiments. Sara was particularly impressed with the miniature jars of preserves and cream cheese. She thought to herself, *Life in the big leagues is pretty sweet.*

As Sara finished getting coffee and halfheartedly putting a few pieces of fruit on a plate (she knew her knotted stomach wouldn't let her eat), Nancy came over. She got her own coffee and a plain bagel, and they walked over to the elegantly appointed navy-blue leather seating area by the window. Nancy was known for her impeccable taste; she was often ribbed about having missed her calling as a world-famous interior designer hosting one of those TV shows on the home and garden channel.

As Nancy got seated, she was half-venting, half trying to break the ice, as she said, "My gosh, my daughter waited until the last minute to finish up her literature paper and we were up last night until God knows what time editing it together. So I told her I'd get here early this morning and email the references I had from my bookshelf while she finished up the proofreading and printing at home. I'm so glad she is a senior this year!" She finished that last sentence with a very audible sigh.

"How do you do it, Nancy? How do you raise kids and run a company? Are there days you just want to run and scream?"

"Oh, Sara, are you kidding? There are *many* days I want to run and scream! But most days I absolutely love it. If my kids were very young I don't think I could do it. But I have a great family and a really understanding husband, and that makes a huge difference. Plus, when you lead a successful company like Brookreme, it's a lot less stressful than running one that's in the dumps." They both laughed.

Nancy got right down to it: "So, it sounds like you and Elliot had a little tussle yesterday, eh?"

Sara rolled her eyes, half smiling, but mostly embarrassed. She could tell Nancy was trying to be warm and helpful, and she was grateful for that. "Yeah, I guess that's what you could call it. Nancy, I'm just so sorry. I was going to call Elliot as soon as it's morning his time and apologize. I don't know what got into me, but before I knew it, I was—"

Nancy stopped her.

"Sara, before you go into all of that, I really do want to understand, from your point of view, what happened. Tell me—honestly—what happened in the meeting."

Sara gathered her thoughts, quickly inventorying all of the options she'd worked out. But somehow, in this moment, looking Nancy in the eye, none of them seemed helpful. So she just dove in.

"Nancy, what happened was . . . I just screwed up. In the heat of all we've been doing, I just wrote down the wrong deadline for my piece of work. These last few days, I've been so distracted by the incredible opportunity you and Nolan offered, all worked up about what to do, that when Elliot asked me for the PR launch data, I was embarrassed. Everyone knows I hate dropping the ball, and I don't do it too often. Somehow, and for the life of me I don't know why, I just couldn't cop to owning it. So I tried to fake my way out of it, and it blew up. And not for nothing, but Elliot just has a way of pushing my buttons. So when he started in on trying to take the work over himself, it just pissed me off. Please don't hear that as trying to blame him. I shouldn't have lost my temper and spoken to him that way. I guess all the stress, and how intense everything is getting this close to launch—I was just wound up too tight and I boiled over—unfortunately, all over Elliot. Nancy, I really am so sorry. And if you want to take back the offer to go to Asia, I'll understand. When I thought about it, it's ironic that I realized how disappointed I would be—not just because my ego would be bruised, but because I think deep down inside I really wanted it but was just scared. That may all be water under the bridge. Elliot probably told you he didn't want me there anyway. I just hope you'll let me keep my job."

Nancy started laughing in a warmhearted way. "You think you're getting off the hook that easily? Not on your life, miss. You may have messed up in a meeting yesterday, but that doesn't change the fact that you are still needed to make this launch successful. We've bet the farm on this. Nothing has changed as far as I'm concerned."

Sara was quite dumbfounded. She didn't know what to say.

"But Nancy, I——"

"But nothing, Sara." Nancy waved her hand. "I know how irritating Elliot can be. I was in Sydney with him a few months ago, and I went off on him too. It wasn't right. I shouldn't have lost my cool either. But he pushed me to the edge and I lost it. I apologized, and so did he. He and I have a great relationship and enough 'give and take' between us that there is deep regard and respect underneath our bantering. I'm sure in time you will have the same relationship with him. He can be a pompous dope sometimes—and I'd say that if he were here in the room—but most of the time he's brilliant and a good guy. When I talked to him last night, he knew he was out of line with you as well. He wasn't at all lobbying to have you off the team. He did raise the concern about your temper, which I think is fair. But more so, he was afraid he put your decision at risk and may have scared you off the team. So he was calling as much to express his frustration with the meeting as he was to ask me to help make sure you still would consider the job. Now, that doesn't change the fact that you behaved incredibly unprofessionally in that meeting, Sara, and if you do that in Asia, you could most definitely put things at risk. We need to figure out how to make sure that doesn't happen. But the invitation is still on the table as far as I'm concerned."

Sara was crying now, and she didn't even try to hide it. She couldn't speak.

"Sara, you are a very gifted woman, and we see that. We want the best for you. You have a promising future with us. But you know you have this really sharp edge to you that doesn't help your credibility. As you grow your career, your ability to form solid relationships with others is going to be a lot more important than having brilliant branding ideas or marketing strategies. Though that's going to be a tough shift for you to make, now is the time to start. And trust me, I know how hard it can be. I've had more than my fair share of difficult conversations with people. I've been pushy. I've been mean. When I was running Europe, I was fondly referred to as the 'bitch on wheels.' I kept a strong exterior upper lip, but inside it hurt like anything. I resented it. But what hurt most is that I knew there was partial truth underneath that crude label. I had to radically change the ways I've led as I've grown through the organization. I didn't want to be known that way. I know I can be hard driving, but I couldn't let that be an excuse. And somehow, though it's highly unfair, when men behave that way, it's overlooked, even encouraged. When women behave like that, we're labeled and discounted. At this stage in my career, I'm starting to understand why. I think for so long, women have felt the need to behave like men to succeed in a nearly all-men corporate world. In many cases, we've given up being women to gain success up the ladder. Years ago, they referred to the 'glass ceiling' that women hit—unable to get past certain rungs on the corporate ladder. Silly concept really, but the metaphor made sense.

"When I got this job, the woman who mentored me on Brookreme's board of directors took me out to dinner and gave me words of advice I've held dearly ever since. She said, 'Nancy, before you are a CEO, you are a woman. You are a mother. You are a wife. You are a sister, a friend. Then, you are a leader, a mentor, a boss, a visionary. And women do those things differently from men. In fact, in some cases we do them better. Don't try and compete on men's terms. At least for the rest of your career, there will probably always be more of them than you. You are a leader and you are a woman. Be proud of both. When you are angry, be angry as a woman gets angry, not as a man gets angry. When you are sad, again, be a woman about it. When you screw up, be a woman about it. Men tell each other to "be a man about it" when life gets tough. I'm telling you to "be a woman about it." And if you are, you will give Brookreme one of the greatest gifts you could ever offer. A leader that is all of herself—talented, smart, imperfect, learning, impatient, tender, driven, anxious—all of which she is . . . as a woman.'"

Sara was mesmerized by Nancy's words. She could hardly believe she was hearing them. It was like someone was finally putting into words things that had long confused and frustrated Sara but that she had never named. She wondered if Nancy saw in her some of the same characteristics of herself from her early career. She would never be so presumptuous to ask, but just the possibility was more than a little flattering.

"Nancy, I don't know why I lose my temper so sharply. I just flare up. I know I'm a perfectionist. I have high standards and I expect a lot of myself, and I expect a lot from others. I know that gets me in hot water sometimes. So when I drop the ball, it's just hard for me to swallow. And when people behave insultingly, I just can't handle it. And if I'm honest about it, I know it's harder when a guy does it. Although, let's be honest, women can be pretty petty, can't we?"

They both laughed with that sense of knowing something all too well.

"Sara, you're going to have to work hard on that perfectionism. You might need to look pretty far back into your life to understand its roots. But it's a nasty little strain that, if you allow it to leak into your leadership, could really cause trouble. Let yesterday be fair warning to you. Even when you think you have things under control, when push comes to shove, you're gonna go down that road unless you learn now what triggers that behavior. For me, I can tell you it had a lot to do with growing up in a very achievement-focused family. We had a doctor, a business executive, a college professor, a computer programmer, and a concert pianist. We weren't a prison camp, don't get the wrong idea. But we were expected to excel. I always felt like everyone else was smarter than me. Everyone else seemed to catch on quicker, get ahead with less effort, and make their grades with half the effort I had to put in. So I vowed I wouldn't be passed over just because I had to work harder. I just worked harder than everyone else.

"The trouble was that when I became a leader, I held everyone else to the same standard. Instead of enjoying the fact that people didn't have to work as hard as I did to get great results, I resented it. And I drove them, making them think even great results could be greater. When I think back to the people I hurt, it makes my stomach sick. I don't want to see you end up that kind of leader. Don't get me wrong, Sara; I'm by no means 'fixed'—I still have a ways to go. But I have worked hard on how I relate to others. And I honestly think I've made good progress. Sure, there are days I slip back into my old terse self. I'm not perfect. But when I mess up, I own it, apologize, and move on. You are very talented, and more often than not you are a fun person to be around. It's clear your colleagues enjoy working with you, though I understand even *they* bristle when your edge shows itself. I'd like to see you nip this in the bud now while your career is still unfolding. I'd hate to see you derail and miss the chance to spread your wings because you have one too many incidents like yesterday."

Sara took a few moments to compose herself. "Nancy, I'm just blown away. I've been desperate for someone to tell me things like this for a long time. I . . . never dreamed it would be you. I've watched you from a distance and I've been fascinated by you. I'm not blowing smoke, Nancy. Really, I've been amazed by your leadership. I knew it had to be harder than it looked, but I couldn't imagine how. I'm grateful you were willing to share this with me. Nancy, I promise you, I will work on this. You know I'm committed to Brookreme. I love this place. Even at its craziest, it's a great company. Who knows where my career's gonna take me. Some days, I just want to go flip burgers. But I know things are gonna get really exciting here, and I think I want a piece of that action."

Sara and Nancy went on to have a rich and meaningful conversation about leadership, about the kinds of situations that set off Sara's dark side, and the kinds of things she might do in those situations. Somehow, her anxiety about Asia had just downgraded significantly. She knew she might mess up, but knowing that Nancy's confidence had not been shaken made a profound difference in her outlook.

"Thanks, Nancy. You just have no idea how much this meant to me. The encouragement, your confidence, and oh, thanks for the ideas on how to build my relationship with Elliot. Those will definitely come in handy."

Sara paused to compose herself for the next question.

"This is going to be a really presumptuous question, and maybe even inappropriate. But I may not get the chance again to ask. When I'm in Asia, if I hit some rocky road, would it be all right . . . would it be ok if . . . I called to get your thoughts or . . . help?" It was a harder question for Sara to ask than even she had thought it would be.

Nancy laughed hard again. "Ahhh, I see asking for help isn't your strong suit either. Good to tackle that one quickly too—you're going to need help and will have to ask for it from everyone around you. To be honest, Sara, I would be disappointed if you *didn't* call me to check in every now and then. Rest assured, if I don't hear from you, I will call *you*. I've got my eye on you. And that's a good thing. Because I believe in you. Don't hide behind your pride and your need to prove anything. We already know you are good. Enjoy being good. And enjoy letting us work together with you to uncover all of the 'not yet' inside you. Deal?"

"Deal." Sara raised her coffee mug in a toast.

Nancy walked Sara to the door. She gave her a hug and said, "You'll be great over there, Sara. I know you will."

Sara smiled and said, "I think it's morning in Sydney now. I have an important call to make. And I'll let Nolan know we spoke, and that it looks like we're on for Asia."

They gave each other the Brookreme ceremonial soft high five and parted ways to start their day.

For the Moments Yet to Come . . .

1. What experiences have you had of leaders coming alongside you and contributing to your own development? Have there been consequences for not having sufficiently good mentors? What have the benefits been from those who have invested in you?

2. Have you been generous with your time to those with whom you lead?

3. How are you intentional about your own leadership formation? What routine activities do you engage in to continually prepare yourself for leadership?

4. How regularly do you consider what contributions you could make to those you lead with? Do the relationships you have with them invite generous participation, or do they need to be strengthened to allow for mutual contribution?

CHAPTER SIX

A GRATEFUL CHAMPION

The Death of Patronizing, The Dare of Gratitude

Gratitude is not only the greatest of virtues,
but parent of all the others.

Cicero

Opportunity: Be more grateful, less complimentary, to sustain courage and endurance.

What if this were your organization?

The tension had mounted in the room like a pressure cooker. Nobody spoke. There was really nothing left to say anyway. Everyone had done everything they could possibly do. Now it was just a waiting game.

The launch reception had been a massive success. The press and media coverage had exceeded expectations. The sales team, led by Lana Hu, had made excellent contacts and set up several key meetings. The bundled solutions concept was definitely turning the heads of key players in the consumer electronics and telecom industry up and down the Pacific Rim.

There was one wrinkle, though. The team thought they'd priced very competitively for a strong entry, but some of the initial reactions of key prospects in early conversations had included some visible apprehension. The team remained convinced that the service and product combination held great value and promise, especially in the highly fragmented telecom space, but price wars could get heated and they didn't want to start something they couldn't finish.

Sara had worked on several pricing models depending on contract length and service agreements. She felt confident each of them could hold their own against Fantronics, whose offerings were still a la carte, bundled only when sold in various combinations by ambitious sales people and discounted just to get the deal signed. Still, she and her teammates couldn't be sure. The looks on some of the faces at the product demo luncheon when the pricing structure was discussed left the Shanghai launch team feeling quite unsettled. They just didn't know what to expect.

The Shanghai office still had an unfinished feel. Some of the furniture was on back order and there were still unpacked boxes in several offices. But the flip charts and diagrams that had hung in the Chicago office war room were now proudly displayed in the Shanghai conference room. It was hard to find really good coffee locally, but the team managed with what they had. Fortunately, someone had had the foresight to ship some beans and grinders to hold them over.

Sara was in her office unpacking and talking to Lisa and some of the new local staff, imagining what the news would be once the sales teams finished up their morning calls. Would they come back with the orders? And if so, would they be good? Enough to get them off on a strong trajectory? Lana had a stunning track record, but would she be able to leverage her knowledge of the culture and bring one in for the team?

Nancy, Don, and Jim were huddled in the corner of the conference room. Don looked excited, Jim was his usual stoic self, and Nancy looked a tad on the anxious side. She had a teleconference scheduled with the analysts in just three hours, and although she had the basic message prepared, she needed word from the sales teams before she could judge how much she could actually say. This was one of the riskiest moves she'd led Brookreme into, and though it wasn't life or death, there was a lot riding on it. Brookreme's previous false starts in Asia had raised skepticism on the street and from the media, and though she had done a fabulous job demonstrating why this strategy would work, the public was still saying, "convince us."

Sara's cell phone rang. It was Lana. Sara covered one ear so she could hear, while the rest of the launch team gathered outside her office, nervously anticipating every possible scenario. Fear and excitement were both palpable. Sara jotted down notes on her pad for a few tense moments, then signed off saying, "Thanks, Lana, see you back here in a bit."

Sara slowly closed her cell phone and looked at all the eyes in her doorway. Nancy's were the widest. Sara thought of that scene where E.T. is standing in a closet full of stuffed animals trying to blend in and not be seen. It took a surprising amount of self-control to refrain from sharing that thought with her CEO.

"Lana thinks they might have signed Xin Hua," Sara finally said. This firm was the largest supplier in Shanghai. Their customers included Micron, Panasonic, Samsung, and Nokia. A deal with them could secure a powerful entry trajectory and substantially lower the barrier for Brookreme in Korea. "She also said she got a call from Michael, who told her that the meeting with Asiantron Limited was—" Sara picked up her notes to read the quote, "so far, so good; it's intense but moving along. So that's the news so far."

People didn't know what to do—cheer or groan. Nancy asked, "What does she mean, she thinks they *might have* signed? Did they or didn't they?"

Sara could see Nancy was on edge. "She said they agreed in principle on terms," she replied, "but the pricing structure needed to be different. Apparently, the bundle they want isn't one we initially anticipated. They liked the idea of a one-stop shop, but for their strategy they need elements of both bundles. So Lana did the best she could to structure something to keep them in the conversation and said she would put together a formal proposal for them by tomorrow morning. She's on her way back here now. Xin Hua was going to be faxing us their estimates for the order today so we could be more precise in our pricing. She said they were—" again she consulted her notes, "enthusiastic and accommodating. So, when Lana gets back here, we'll get to work on putting together the deal for them. I think this seems very positive, don't you?"

The moment the words were out of her mouth, Sara wondered if this was the question to ask at this juncture.

All eyes were on Nancy now to see if she felt the same way.

"Oh, absolutely," Nancy replied without skipping a beat. "Just to get this far in the process after everyone's hard work and months of preparation is a win for us." There was a hint of relief in the air, as she continued, with a slight tongue-in-cheek tone, "Obviously, a signed deal would really make my day. But at this point I'll take any good news we can get. And this is definitely good news. Nice work, everyone."

For some, that last comment took a bit of wind out of their sails. People who'd been hard at the grind for months wondered if Nancy really understood what was behind the "nice work." Did she really understand the exhausting hours, the tenacious networking and scheduling, the competitive intelligence, the market testing, retesting, and re-retesting, the focus groups, the reception planning and brand image building, the technological and scientific R&D needed to make sure these new offerings could work in Asia—especially China—without a hitch? Did she register the personal sacrifices of family time and social lives required to get Brookreme here on such an aggressive time-line? Everyone knew the high stakes associated with this venture, and that caused some anxiety about careers and futures. Some people were realizing that they were as anxious about Brookreme succeeding in Asia as they were about failure. If everything panned out, would they really be *appreciated* for all they'd done? Was it even known? Would people just get some token piece of Lucite for their office, etched with a trivial statement like "Congratulations for a successful Asia launch"? It was hard to guess which letdown would hurt more.

Nancy was working with Don on her messaging to the analysts, trying to figure out how to leverage these fragments of information into something that was newsworthy but did not overstimulate expectations. This was a delicate line to walk. Nancy reminisced for a moment about the first conversation she'd had with the team nearly eight months earlier. She and Don chuckled, remember-ing the argument they'd had afterward.

"We've come a long way since then, haven't we?" Nancy reflected.

Don nodded in agreement, with a long and knowing, "Ohhhh, yes."

"I hope you hear this in the spirit I mean, Don," Nancy said. "I want you to know that I'm proud of you. I know this role has not been easy. You've had to grow into these shoes much faster than most leaders. I've pushed you hard—sometimes too hard—and still you've risen to the occasion. I've seen you work hard, not just on your projects, but on becoming the kind of leader I know you want to be, and it has impressed me. It may not seem like I've noticed, and for that I'm sorry. But I have been watching. And whatever hap-pens here today, I want you to know how grateful I am for the tireless work you and this team have put in here. I know—I really know—what it's cost you. Thank you." Nancy put her head down briefly as the emotion of that moment caught her by surprise.

It caught Don by surprise even more. "Wow, Nancy. That means a lot to me. Maybe more than you know. To be honest, I wasn't sure if you understood the toll this was taking to achieve. But I also knew whether or not you noticed wasn't the point. I wanted to get the job done. We did what we had to do. Just the same, the encouragement means a lot. Coming from you, it feels especially good to hear."

Nancy just looked up and smiled.

"Nancy, while we're on this, let me ask you a favor. I know it's not your style, but I can only imagine it would mean the world to this team if they heard that from you too. You've joked a lot about public displays of emotion—'PDE' as you call it—and how you avoid them at all cost." They both laughed, and Don continued, "But that kind of genuine appreciation would go a long way with this team. They know they've done a good job. They don't need to hear that. What they need to know is that all they've done matters, regardless of what happens today. Yes, of course some signed deals would make it feel a whole lot better. But even if we don't get them today, they will come eventually. And they need to know that all their sweat and sacrifice matters now. You think you'd be up for it?"

Nancy smiled. She knew she had no choice, and looked at Don with her wry grin and slight nod, indicating a lot without words—she would do it, it would be hard for her, and she was glad he had asked. They did the soft high five. Don tossed a package of tissues at Nancy and said, "Here, looks like you need these. God forbid you break your track record of no PDEs." He winked.

Lana had returned with her team and was huddled in Sara's office. Calculators were humming, spreadsheets were printing, and laptops were being pounded on throughout the suite of offices. There was a laser-sharp focus on getting the proposal reconfigured. Lana was hoping to assemble a beautiful package and have it delivered by courier before the end of the day. She couldn't add her usual touch of Godiva chocolates and wine like she did with her California clients, because in China gifts were not a part of business protocol. But she could make the package look beautiful and she could get it to them earlier than she had promised.

She was a class act and everyone could easily see why she was the company's top sales person. Nancy could hear the precision and energy with which she was directing the team, and the extraordinary synergy between Lana and Sara as they crunched numbers and brainstormed how to make the deal work for both Xin Hua and Brookreme.

Nancy slid behind Lana at a moment when she was not near anyone else, and whispered in her ear, "You are amazing. Just amazing." Lana knew it was Nancy's voice, but turned to look in surprise. She grinned from ear to ear and said quietly, "Thanks, Nancy. Thanks a lot." Lana had thought it was really cool that Nancy had flown over with some of her team for the launch to lend support and help. There were only a few cynics who thought she'd come to inspect and spy. Most understood she was there to offer a hand in any way she could.

Lana and Sara called Don, Jim, and Nancy in and ran the deal structure by them to get their input and buy-in. There was some debate and some more brainstorming. Nancy enjoyed being part of the team and getting the chance to play in the field. It had been many years since she'd been on the ground building deals. She actually had some insights and ideas that strengthened the proposal and made the deal more attractive for Xin Hua. Lana suggested that she and Nancy both personally deliver the proposal at the end of the day, which she believed would really help close the deal. Nancy gladly agreed.

As they finished the discussion, the team went back to putting the final touches on the proposal. The cover bore both the Xin Hua and Brookreme logo.

Beneath the energetic hubbub, there was an unfamiliar noise that most ignored. Sara came out into the hallway and shushed everyone to listen more closely. It was a strange beeping noise. They all looked at each other with curiosity—they didn't recognize it, but whatever it was, it was coming from the reception area. Lana came out into the hallway and saw Sara's inquisitive look that was clearly referring to the odd noise. Without any expression, she simply explained, "It's the fax machine."

For the Moment

How do you typically show gratitude?

How do you deal with your own public displays of emotion? Avoid them? Temper them?

How could Nancy show genuine gratitude, even if the fax machine is bearing bad news?

Are you able to experience gratitude in the face of disappointment?

William James said, "The deepest craving of human nature is the need to be appreciated." Regardless of whether you agree, it is certain that we all desire to be seen as significant and to know our contributions matter. Otherwise we wouldn't strive as hard as we do to win the veneration of those leaders we serve. Oddly, today's leaders seem to do one of two things that frustrate this craving. Some withhold their gratitude, feeling that people shouldn't be thanked for just doing their job. Others feel it's important to express thanks, but they use gratitude's cheaper counterfeit, the superficial compliment. "Way to go," "Nice job," "Home run," and countless more appreciative platitudes fill the offices of organizations, and they've left a lot of hollow souls in their wake.

Don't get me wrong. Compliments are nice. For a fleeting moment they feel good. They are just too easily mistaken for gratitude.

> You have to be 100 percent behind someone, before you
> can stab them in the back.
>
>   DAVID BRENT, *regional manager* WERNHAM HOGG
>   *The Office*

HOW COMPLIMENTS CREATE DISTANCE

There's a paradox about compliments. Once bestowed, they often create a separation between the giver and receiver instead of drawing them closer. A boss pays a compliment to someone, and there is an awkward moment. The payer of the compliment has no risk. It is safe to admire the work of others from afar. The receiver must wonder about the degree to which the compliment is sincere. Though probably well-meaning, does the payer of the compliment really understand what was behind the contribution? What it took to make? And more important, have they expressed what the contribution meant to *them* personally?

Too often the answer is no, which means that "atta boy" or "atta girl" frequently feels empty to the receiver. The giver can check off the "I complimented their work" box and move on. The receiver, on the other hand, walks away ambivalent—enjoying the pat on the back, yet second-guessing how much to really enjoy it. This isn't much better than having the giver simply withhold all expression of gratitude and having the receiver feel ambivalent about how the boss sees the work accomplished.

Many years ago, I was sitting around a table talking with a group of friends. We were all talking about our fathers. My father was killed by a drunk driver when I was working in Europe. I was just twenty-one years old at the time. Three weeks earlier, around Thanksgiving, I'd called home to talk to my family and we were all excited about my upcoming trip home for Christmas. On that phone call, my father said what ended up being the last words he'd ever say to me. He was a typical Italian man of few words, so compliments were never his forte. But he paid me one, and I cherished it for a long time. To me, those words were the validating sentiments every son wants to hear. When I shared them proudly with my friends at the table, all they returned were blank stares. One said to me, "And you thought that was a good thing?" Another said, "Scraps look good when the pickings are thin." In an instant my entire relationship with my father had been reframed. Did I know my father was grateful for and proud of me? Of course. I heard him tell everyone and anyone he could. I lived vicariously through those words. But now these morsels of accolade needed to be seen in a new light. I could still cherish them. But I could also grieve that over the course of my life, they were too few, and, as it turned out, the last was offered not a moment too soon.

I tell you this story not to invite your sympathy, but to ask you to consider the cost of withholding your gratitude from those friends, loved ones, and colleagues that matter most to you. I loved my father very much, and I know he loved me. I will never know how different my life would have been had he been more generous with his gratitude. But I do know how different my relationship with my son and daughter will be because of it. Those words of my father's, for the moment, drew us close. But later, they created a distance because they had not ascended from gratitude-rich soil. Seeing that relationship through the eyes of generous friends enabled great change in my life.

So here is the difference between a compliment and gratitude. A *compliment* is a generic acknowledgment of something tangible—a completed task, a nice tie, a persuasive presentation, or a kind gesture. *Gratitude* goes beyond the compliment to the intangible *why* you are thankful for the completed task or the persuasive presentation, the *personal* effect the tangible act had on you, and your *genuine curiosity* about what it took for the tangible act to be accomplished. People are always glad to have their work acknowledged, to know that it matters in the abstract. But to know that it matters to *you* is something more. To know that you are interested in how they made their contribution—regardless of how large or small—by inquiring of them how they did it, signals a level of honor and gratitude that transcends a compliment.

Compliments acknowledge something concrete—a what. Gratitude acknowledges the contribution as an extension of the contributor, a reflection of who they are, and an honoring of the giver as much as the gift. Think about it. At those moments you felt most honored by a leader, wasn't it knowing they *personally* regarded your work and were genuinely interested in your achievement that made the moments mean something to you?

Of course, what I am suggesting requires emotional risk. As you saw with Nancy at Brookreme, for many leaders, public displays of emotion (PDE) are often socially unacceptable in today's workplace. Today's leaders worry that displays of emotion will make them appear dependent on others and weak. Compliments are an act of intellect—simple, clear, and concise. Gratitude, however, is an act of both intellect and heart, requiring emotion. Emerging leaders know this well, and for that reason they typically reject compliments as insincere before they're even finished. This rejection may be visible to the leader paying the compliment, who will feel the emerging leader is downright rude. Another ugly cycle.

Ironically, an act motivated by kind intensions and desire for a good relationship can actually create distance between leaders. Compliments subtly remind others you have the power to validate their work, or at least you believe you do. Many people consider shallow, uninformed compliments—the worst kind—as nothing more than patronizing attempts by the giver to look like a good leader. Cheap compliments, especially from a typically harsh leader, invite resentment and disbelief.

To eliminate the negative residue compliments can inadvertently engender, you must have a genuinely appreciative heart and be seen as a grateful champion by others. And to do that, you have to allow the fingerprints of others' contributions to visibly mark you. The generative process of gratitude—the known and seen impact people have on one another—is the glue that transforms an organization into a vibrant, high-performing community.

> *"Bus driver,* move that bus*!"*
> Ty Pennington and fifteen million weekly fans
> of *Extreme Makeover: Home Edition*

Why Gratitude Requires Community to Thrive

For millions of fans, ABC's blockbuster show *Extreme Makeover: Home Edition* is a source of inspiration. What keeps us on the edge of our seats is knowing we are about to see that week's fortunate family jumping around, screaming at the top of their lungs, crying, falling to their knees, falling into each other's arms, shouting in shock and disbelief—all at the sight of their new home, built in just seven days by hundreds of volunteers from their community. The new home is hidden from view by a bus until Pennington and the crowd of onlookers command the driver to move it. The electric rush that surges through everyone watching as we see the family's faces is indescribable. But we can name it. It is *gratitude.*

   Tragic stories of terminal illnesses, deaths of parents and children, unforeseen injuries disabling a household's only breadwinner, caring families who have adopted underprivileged children but lacked sufficient space to care for them, handicapped children unable to thrive in inadequate environments . . . all of these are transformed in just a week to stories of hope, promise, and inspiration. The tears on the faces of the design team and volunteers tell it all. *They* are the ones who feel grateful to be part of changing the lives of others. *They* tell of the blessing they have received to work on the home of a family in their community. These people have worked tirelessly and selflessly in shifts around the clock for seven days to complete the house. The family benefiting from this work often struggles to find words to express the gratitude they are feeling. They comment throughout the viewing of their home how "there just aren't words," or "I just don't know what to say," or "just saying 'thank you' seems so small." As a good friend of mine describes it, it is like a crescendo of gratitude. Each side trying to out-thank the other. "Thank you." "No, thank *you!*" "No, really, thank *you.*" What a great problem to have—who can out-bless whom!

So what makes this phenomenon work? Why do our souls swell with anticipation and hope at the thought of seeing faces and lives transformed by the kindness of others? I believe it is the sacred element of community. If we accept the underlying premise that fundamental transformation—be it personal or organizational—happens only in the context of relationship, then it stands to reason that the experience of that transformation must be among networks of many relationships, or a *community.* There is a wondrous marvel, a force that happens among communities when they join together to work toward a common outcome. Organizations that learn to cultivate this force and leaders who learn to shepherd others into their place in the community, tend to achieve the extraordinary results only communities can produce.

This is a place where incumbent leaders can learn much from emerging leaders. Incumbent leaders grew up in an era characterized by hyperindividualism. By contrast, emerging leaders have a more natural inclination toward community. In their book, *Creating Community Anywhere,* Carolyn Shaffer and Kristin Anundsen offer this insightful thought from Juanita Brown, co-originator of the World Café, mentioned in Chapter Two:

"Modern organizations have separated us from our traditional ties to the land, to our families, to the community, and perhaps most importantly, from the connection to our own spirit. In this process, many have been cut off from our hearts' desire—to be part of a larger community of endeavor that is worthy of our best efforts."

What Brown is suggesting is that our desire for community is innate and that our best efforts thrive in the context of community. I would go further and suggest that our best efforts *perpetuate themselves* in the context of the gratitude of that community.

> *Don't it always seem to go, that you don't know what you've got 'til it's gone?*
>
> JONI MITCHELL
> *"Big Yellow Taxi"*

In Harm's Way: Choosing Gratitude Before Tragedy

I find it odd that crisis seems to commonly precede the greatest levels of gratitude people experience. In organizations, I find it especially peculiar that valuable employees are most appreciated after they submit their resignation. Suddenly, leaders are able to produce all kinds of appreciation and recognition, the need for which seemed to strangely elude them prior to the key player's decision to go. Contributions and talents that went unnoticed come directly under the spotlight as leaders desperately woo people to stay. What if those same people had experienced that level of regard *before* the notion to leave ever entered their mind? This isn't an idle question. Recent research by Sirota Consulting of Purchase, New York, found that unhappiness with the way things are at work is the biggest factor provoking early departures. Interestingly enough, this ranked ahead of actual confrontation with the boss or coworkers or complaints about pay. Based on interviews with workers, the Sirota survey found that only a third of those who planned to quit in less than a year said they were satisfied with their overall working conditions. Of those who said they'd stay for five years or more, 85 percent were satisfied. Satisfaction with salary was the least significant factor between those likely to leave and those committed to staying. I've seen the data in this report translate into the surprise leaders have when key workers who "ought to know" how much they are valued by virtue of their compensation packages resign anyway. They realize too late that the key employee needed something more than just the paycheck to feel fulfilled at work.

To further illustrate the power of gratitude *even in tragedy,* consider the countless stories of people's responses to grave calamities—how they are able to move forward with their lives because in the midst of their anguish they found blessings for which to be thankful. In my introduction to this book, I mentioned how my then-employer, Marsh and McLennan, responded to the tragedy of September 11, 2001, pulling together to shoulder the losses our colleagues suffered that day. There are many examples of gratitude's power in people's experiences of that event. Here's just one:

Lyz Glick's husband, Jeremy, was one of the heroes of September 11. He is believed to be one of the men who overpowered hijackers on United Flight 93, causing it to crash into a Pennsylvania field instead of its intended target. Today, she says she has no regrets. Instead, she is filled with gratitude for the way she and Jeremy celebrated the life they had together. "[In our final phone call] the first thing he said was, 'There's some bad people on the plane.' We talked for twenty minutes, but we were able to find peace in having an emotional connection with one another. We just started saying 'I love you' over and over again. We must have said it for five minutes. It was like a light went on in my body of love, and I [thought], 'Okay, I can do this. I can be strong for him. I'm very grateful that I did have that last conversation with Jeremy, and that it wasn't a conversation that was filled with panic and fear. It really brought our relationship full circle, and it showed the type of husband that Jeremy was, and the type of relationship that we had. He wanted to prepare me for a life without him. He told me that he needed me to be happy in my life, and to take care of [our daughter] Emerson, and he would be supportive of any decisions that we had made. As every day goes forward, [that conversation] brings me just that much more peace. When it happened, I don't think I really realized the power of those words. It reminds me of how much he loved me, that in such a terrible time . . . he could think of me. I think that's one of the greatest gifts he could have given me. I think life is a gift, and I have two choices. I can either not embrace my life and live in the past, or I can look at things that I was thankful for in this relationship. I thank God that I did have five years of marriage. And I have a daughter. We didn't take time for granted. We were able to do more in five years of marriage than many people are able to do in a lifetime. The morning after it happened, I remember looking at [Emerson] and feeling sorry for her for not knowing Jeremy . . . Then something clicked in my head. I said, 'I'm not going to let that happen.' I want to have joy in my life. There has to be a lesson learned from this. I want to look back on my life and know that I don't have regrets. I lost the most important person in my life, but I was able to go on. And I want him to look down from Heaven and be proud of me."

I hope you have your own inventory of stories chronicling gratitude that moved you through the most difficult moments of life. But more than that, I hope that gratitude will become more than a response to tragedy, or a way to survive tragedy. What if gratitude were simply a way of life? What if we approached leadership as a posture of indebtedness instead of a posture of entitlement? I think organizational performance would see utterly profound results.

How many buses have you moved for those in your organization? How have you used your leadership in the service of transforming those around you? And when buses have been moved for you, revealing significant achievement as a result of your organization's heroic efforts, how well did you show your community gratitude and awe?

Every day in organizations, acts of sacrificial heroism go unnoticed. True, people aren't building brand new homes in seven days as a matter of course, but the dedication they show to the cause for which they are working and the inspiration they hope to rouse in others are the same. Whether you are the bus driver moving the bus, or the family behind the bus waiting for something extraordinary to be revealed, awakening gratitude in your organization should be a routine part of your day.

Here's why. Daily, people put themselves in harm's way to produce acts of heroism. They risk political harm when they advance your agenda at the expense of your organizational nemesis. They risk harming their reputation when they put their ideas on the line to be scrutinized by you and others. They risk harm to relationships—from colleagues as well as their family and friends who must also make sacrifices that enable them to perform. They risk harm from you—when you are callous, grumpy, stubborn, aloof, intimidating, uninformed, biased, manipulative, indecisive, unprepared, angry, curt, moody, self-serving, self-promoting, insecure, paranoid, or impulsive. (Admit it—at least one of those words has had your name on it at one time or another.) We ask those we lead to return day after day and put themselves in harm's way on behalf of our organizations—and this should evoke the greatest degree of indebtedness possible. Gratitude should be our foremost response, and we should shower it on others whenever we can.

One business unit president of a large building materials manufacturer I spoke with had these thoughts to offer:

> Every day I am amazed at what these people can do. We ask so much of them, and really, if you think about it, give them relatively

little with which to accomplish all we ask. It is their spirit, their inge-
nuity, their determination, that gets these pallets loaded and shipped
every day, week in, week out. I've watched them fight zealously for
our customers to get their shipments on time. I've watched them go
to the mat for each other. One guy's wife had cancer last year, and
the entire region chipped in money to make sure he could be home
with her. I made sure the company matched their contribution. It
was just the right thing to do. But it came from them. When times
have been lean, they've voluntarily taken pay cuts so we didn't have
to lay anyone off. Now that times are booming, they are willing to do
whatever it takes to keep the business moving, to get the orders in
and filled on time. I have a friend that I golf with who tells me his
people complain all the time no matter what he does. I asked how
often he thanked them for what they contributed, and he said, 'Well,
I guess not enough.' I tell these people every day how much I appreciate them. I write them notes and put them in their locker. I call
them at home at the end of a rough day when I know they had to
really press hard. This is a hard business. It's competitive like a street
fight. But then I guess what business isn't? I don't have to 'make it
up' when I tell them I'm thankful. I really am amazed by them. And
I know I don't deserve to have people this dedicated. I may try to be
a good leader—to care about them, to give them chances to show
what they can do, to be fair and pay them as well as I can. But in the
end, this is the kind of dedication any president dreams about having. And I will do whatever I must to protect that dedication. I won't
tolerate any disrespect or nonsense among any departments. And
they know it. But I've never really worried about that. There's just an
unspoken understanding here. We value each other. And we don't
mind telling each other. We have each other's back. And we are very
grateful for the team around us that has ours. You can't put a price
on that. Every leader ought to be this fortunate.

I don't mind admitting how good it does my soul to hear leaders express such spirited regard for others. When we too often take
for granted the contributions of others—especially those who
enable us to do our jobs—it's heartening to know that leaders like
this one won't succumb to the temptation of overlooking their colleagues. They understand that when it comes to sustaining others'
courage and endurance, being a grateful champion has no substitute. Unfortunately, not all leaders learn this lesson easily, and
leave in their wake the remnants of ingratitude. If the most excit-

ing stories in our research were about dreaming, the most exasperating were about ingratitude and the cost of being disregarded.

Joshua, an enthusiastic ad executive, told us about his manager. Joshua was asked to head up a new project for which he had direct experience in the product category. He worked efficiently and effectively to organize resources, set schedules, manage the workflow, and deliver the proposal on time. Indeed, he should have earned the respect of his manager. Instead, Joshua recounts, "After a few weeks, my leader came to me one evening and said he was worried because he didn't see enough 'panic' in the office. People weren't staying late every night. The office was too neat. There was not enough flurry of activity. He concluded that 'we must not be working hard enough.' I explained that since this was a product I knew well, he should be concerned if there was a panic . . . not the lack of it. Not convinced, I assigned one person to stay late and make copies and do word processing each night so that the 'leader' in the corner office could see the semblance of panic . . . which eventually became the real thing." Joshua's boss missed the point entirely. The result was higher personnel cost, increased panic, and Joshua's eventual departure to another agency, even after a successful product launch. Indeed, the cost of ingratitude can be far greater than whatever can be dropped to the bottom line.

For the Moment

When have you known "grateful champions" in your life and work?

When have you been guilty of ingratitude?

What advice would you have for Joshua? For his boss?

GRATITUDE'S FAR-REACHING POWER

Gary Haugen is president and CEO of International Justice Mission (IJM), a Washington, D.C.–based NGO whose mission is to rescue and help the oppressed around the world who have become victims of ruthless injustice. His people literally put themselves in harm's way daily, risking their lives to liberate young children from the enslavement of human trafficking, to rescue wrongfully imprisoned men and women from the torturous confines of corrupt prisons, and to face off with the most evil, entrenched perpetrators of exploitation. The trafficking of young children into the sex-for-profit industry is one of the most lucrative criminal industries. The FBI estimates that the sex trafficking industry generates revenue of around $9.5 billion annually. In his book *Terrify No More*, Gary tells the story of his team's dangerous, heroic rescue of children from the brothels of Cambodia. He offers these words: "My deepest gratitude is extended to my IJM colleagues who do the work and make the life choices that give us these stories to tell. The true depth of their courage and generosity is seen only in secret by their Maker but in these years I have been granted sufficient glimpses of such authentic goodness and glory that I now hold a storehouse of stories for my grandchildren when I walked with real, flesh-and-blood heroes."

I spoke with Gary about what it was like to be a leader, knowing your dearest colleagues faced grave harm to accomplish the mission of the organization, and about what gratitude meant for him. He had this to say:

> I think my first job is to make sure I am grounded in reality. Gratitude, genuine gratitude, has to acknowledge that the accomplishment of our mission has little to do with me personally. I think it's a little bit funny that any leader would assume their own contribution to be overwhelmingly tied to the results an organization achieves. The gratitude comes when the reality hits me that all I am credited for and all that is attributed to me is really from others—if leaders don't get that, then we aren't in touch with reality. We bring tangible rescue to victims of injustice, and justice to perpetrators, and help to communities who are suffering. How much of that do I actually affect? Those results come from those in the field. I get to tell the story, rally enthusiasm and support, rally good leaders around us, but I don't get those results. I understand my value is in serving my people who are actually doing the work. That yields very authentic gratitude for the team. Gratitude also makes me want to be better at my job. I want to serve them well because I am so

thankful for them. I want to be better at my job because they are unbelievable at what they do. They are an inspiration for pursuing excellence in my job. I'm not necessarily grateful for the utility of what they do, extraordinary though it is. What cheers my heart the most is who they are as people. They have incredible character, passion, and commitment. They are *grateful* for the privilege to make the sacrifices they make and serve those who are hurting. They put themselves in harm's way because of the kind of people they are. They don't count the cost. They can't believe they get to go and do this work they love to do, dangerous though it sometimes is. I'm awed by their passion and drive to care for the things that are really hard to care about. How could I not be grateful every day in my job? I am moved daily to thankfulness, and I want to tell them all the time. Some struggle to receive it, but I tell them anyway. I want them to know what I think is wonderful about them. My job is to slow things down long enough to celebrate, and be grateful for, the extraordinary work that emerges from the ordinariness of what we do every day. They are joyfully choosing what they do—the price they are willing to pay for doing something that really matters. The greatest pain we do bear—together—is that of those who are hurting, suffering, being exploited. The greatest joy is that we get to go do something about it. In many ways, we're so incredibly thankful that we get to go and do it, that we're not all that mindful of our own struggles.

> *If the only prayer you said in your whole life was "thank you," that would suffice.*
> MEISTER ECKHART, *German mystic*

THE BRIDGE TO RELATIONSHIP: SATURATE THOSE WITH WHOM YOU LEAD IN GRATITUDE THAT INSPIRES ENDURING COURAGE

Candidly, I will say that I struggle with the notion of offering ideas on how to be a grateful champion. I've wondered if this is something that can be learned or whether it must emanate from one's character. I haven't reached any firm conclusions, but I would suggest that if you aren't by nature a person of genuine gratitude—if you aren't stirred by the magnificence in those around you and moved easily to thankfulness—you should examine why that is so. I think gratitude ought to be more common than ungratefulness and, frankly, require less effort.

Annie Dillard expresses this better than most in her book *Pilgrim at Tinker Creek*. She writes, "I've been thinking about seeing. There are lots of things to see, unwrapped gifts and free surprises." She's talking about gifts in nature, but there are free gifts in our offices as well. Dillard goes on to tell the story of how, as a young girl, she would "hide" pennies along the sidewalks near her home, and would delight in the thought of the "first lucky passer-by who would receive . . . regardless of merit, a free gift from the universe." Later she adds, "The world is fairly studded and strewn with pennies cast broadside from a generous hand. But—and this is the point—who gets excited by a mere penny?" What if you did?

Maybe we don't see because we aren't looking. Or maybe we're so committed to our own agenda that we ignore the free gifts right in front of us. What if you committed to seeing them and being grateful? I believe it is something far deeper and more systemic that we should continuously work at. Selfishness can root its way into our lives and settle in as a higher level of self-involvement than we would ever care to admit. But the degree to which we are absorbed in ourselves—our issues, our pain, our ambitions, our rights—is the extent to which we crowd out capacity to focus on others. And once there, self-involvement requires a lot more effort to maintain than does caring for others.

Does this mean we should never care for ourselves? Of course not. Self-care is part of good leadership. But we forfeit the experience of community when we don't routinely show those with whom we lead how to regard and value others, trusting that the gratitude, and the championing of our own causes, will return to us from them. Again, Dillard says it well: "It is dire poverty indeed when a man is so malnourished and fatigued that he won't stoop to pick up a penny. But if you cultivate a healthy poverty and simplicity, so that finding a penny will literally make your day, then, since the world is in fact planted in pennies, you have with your poverty bought a lifetime of days. It is that simple. What you see is what you get."

My hunch is that your story of leadership has painted this portrait in both beautiful and unpleasant ways. If you are an incumbent leader, undoubtedly you have overlooked the good in emerging leaders around you. And if you are an emerging leader, the same is true for the incumbent leaders with whom you lead. Keep each other's faces in mind as you read. To those images, I would offer these reflections.

1. *Put on your "gratitude mojo."* Turn gratitude from an Emily Post platitude to an attitude with teeth. Make it cool to be grateful. Because it is. It is the fuel that propels performance and passion. But it's always those basics that so easily get sidestepped. Like the old quip about the man who reacted in shock when handed divorce papers—"But I told you I loved you when we got married"—taking others for granted can come with a high price. Find every reason you can to thank others for who they are, what they bring, and what they contribute. Never fake it. Heed John F. Kennedy's words, "As we express our gratitude, we must never forget that the highest appreciation is not to utter words, but to live by them."

2. *Move buses.* There are opportunities around you—for every customer, for every new employee, for every achievement, at the discovery of every solution, to reveal transformation. Even the smallest of changes is to be celebrated. When people reach new plateaus, don't miss the opportunity to move the bus and reveal that achievement to others. And behind the bus, be the first one screaming wildly (in whatever form looks best on you) in gratitude for what has been revealed.

3. *Inventory what you are grateful for.* And if the list is hard for you to create, you should worry. You wouldn't be where you are were it not for the champions who guided you there. Those champions may have been mentors, friends, family, or your esteemed colleagues with whom you work. Become more grateful for all that has conspired to aid you by taking stock of it. Oprah once had much of the country keeping gratitude journals. That thought may have some of you rolling your eyes, but the results were astounding. The level of joy and gratification those journal keepers lived with says a lot about the power of gratitude and counting one's blessings. If you struggle with assuming that people should just be grateful to have a job and not need any more appreciation than that, you are

grossly misguided in your view of gratitude. You should revamp those views, understand their origins, and rethink your need to be grateful to others and their contributions.

4. *Pay it forward.* Out of your gratitude for the contributions leaders have made to your life, seek out opportunities to give to others. Regardless of whether you are a seasoned leader or an emerging leader of minimal experience, somewhere you have something to offer someone. Figure out where that is, and see if you can't form a relationship in which your contribution might be invited, further perpetuating gratitude.

5. *Harness lessons from tragedy.* At some point, an absence of gratitude has cost you. The loss of a valuable employee, the lack of needed commitment in a crunch from your team, a distinct dearth of hands in the air when soliciting volunteers for a vital project, perhaps even the loss of health of a leader who gave too much. These misfortunes would be sad enough on their own. To repeat them because you didn't learn from them would be catastrophic. Experience in itself doesn't produce learning. *Reflecting* on one's experience does. Stop and reflect on these painful intersections to more deeply understand how a lack of gratitude may have played a part in the unwanted outcome.

6. *Be curious about others' work.* One of the most grateful questions I think a leader can ask is "Can you tell me how you did that?" Provide people a platform to be honored by the community by being able to talk about a particular contribution and what it meant for them to contribute. Affirm how that contribution is an extension of who they are by telling them specifically what it meant to you and how you see it as a reflection of them.

7. *Create community.* The social fabric of an organization is the glue that keeps all the moving parts moving in a cohesive direction. Be sure you are playing host to fun experiences in which the socialization process can move beyond the content of work. Establish an ethos that lets people be "whole people" together and enjoy getting to know each other outside the context of conducting business. Create social rituals that bring people together at regular intervals just for fun. The venue or menu need not be extravagant. The satisfying experience of community will be extravagant enough.

8. *Notice what you notice.* And just as importantly, notice what you don't. Your eyes are trained to see, and you have been condi-

tioned to see those things over and over. Are you quick to draw attention to what could have been better? Are people's shortcomings front and center to you? As we discussed in the last chapter, holding all four views of the diamond at once is essential for you to experience true gratitude. You must be grateful for both the gem and the coal that is forming it. Do you notice your own giftedness, or are you inclined to dwell only on your limitations? When others affirm you, are you gracious, thanking them for their kindness, or are you quick to turn their acknowledgment away? If your eyes have been conditioned not to see what you could be grateful for, in yourself and others, what might you do to retrain your eyes?

As we return for one last visit with our friends at Brookreme, I hope you are sensing positive anticipation for their story. But even more, I hope you are positively anticipating your own leadership story and where it will go from here. Just as the story of Brookreme has had ups and downs, twists and turns, so has yours. I hope you see more clearly now how much influence you have over some of those twists and turns—through the relationships you form with those you lead. And as you reflect on your history, and look ahead to your unfolding story, do so with gratitude.

Now let's see what was on that fax.

Lana pulled the pages out of the fax machine one at a time, shuffling through them. It was clear she knew what she was looking for. When the last page came off, she clenched her eyes shut tightly. It was hard to tell if she was elated or completely let down. She looked up and handed the fax to Nancy, who also read through it just as quickly, also looking for something specific.

This was a level of dramatic tension none of the team had ever experienced. It was almost as if the entire future of the organization was riding on this one order. Of course that wasn't the case, but you couldn't tell that from the faces of those staring eagerly at Nancy as she read. To them, life itself hung in the balance. If this had been a movie, this would be the part where the camera would start moving in slow motion, with deeply moving, inspirational orchestra music rising to a crescendo in the background, panning the room face by face, then back to Nancy as she looked up and her face melted into ecstasy.

"Xin Hua wants to sign for three years, making us their preferred supplier," she said with deep relief.

The room broke into pandemonium like New Year's Eve in Times Square at midnight. Sara was hooting and high-fiving anyone she could get near. Lana was crying overjoyed tears. Even Jim was laughing uproariously. Don was giving hugs to everyone.

Someone popped the corks on several bottles of champagne and poured paper cups for everyone to toast. Before the toast, Nancy had to insert a twinge of caution into the room by reminding them that, "Of course, it is contingent upon the revised proposal that Lana and I deliver to them this evening," and she winked at Lana. With that, they raised their paper cups—which might as well have been fine crystal, given the delight in the room—and Nancy said, "To Brookreme, Asia, and the amazing team of you who got us here!" And everyone drank and went back to the boisterous joy of celebrating.

Nancy looked around the room at the electrically lit up faces of this team. She was overcome with a sense of awe and gratitude for what they had done and how brilliantly they had done it. She caught Don's eye, and he looked back, nodding, to remind her of his request. She hadn't forgotten what he'd asked her to do, but she was just feeling uncomfortable. She always feared that public praise and acknowledgment from leaders came across as phony, because that's what she had seen in her career. Still, she knew she needed to try. She grabbed one of the plastic knives from the counter and started tapping the side of her paper cup with it. It wasn't crystal, but everybody saw her and eventually quieted down.

Nancy began, "I'd like to ask the core launch team led by Don to join me up here, please." Sara, Lana, and the others made their way to the front of the room, and Nancy continued. "None of us will ever understand what it took for this team to pull off this achievement. It's been in the works for many years, long before this team formed about eight months ago. This moment has been brewing inside each of these people their entire lives. And it's been unfolding at Brookreme for many years, as many who have gone before us to bravely pioneer this trail will attest.

"One of my favorite quotes is from Goethe, who said, 'At the moment of commitment, the universe conspires to assist you.' Well, this team is great evidence of that truth. Each of them committed without reservation, and without looking back, to getting us a foothold in Asia. Their genius, their creativity, their perseverance, and their unwavering passion paved the way for us to arrive at this moment. And those characteristics were growing inside each of them well before we met them. But today we are all benefiting from who they each are as professionals, as colleagues, and as friends."

Nancy then looked at each of them down the line one by one. "Not to put anyone on the spot, but I for one would love to hear what this journey has meant to each of you: what you've learned, what was fun, what was hard, and—so we can all grow from your investment—just how the hell you did it! Because of your dedication, Brookreme will never be the same. We've been a strong company. And now we will be stronger. We will touch people and organizations in an entirely new part of the world. And your leadership—individually and collectively—is what brought us here. So I'm going to grab a seat over here, and let you fight over who gets to go first."

They laughed a bit awkwardly and looked at each other, and a few in the room got them some stools and chairs to sit on. Then, one by one, they each told their story of getting to Asia. They thanked one another, thanked Don for his ongoing support, and thanked Nancy for having the vision to believe Brookreme could succeed. They told of the hard moments of failure, of conflict and tension. Sara smiled at Elliot as she acknowledged her own personal growth with patience, at which many giggled with delight. Lana got emotional again and cried, reflecting on her time at Brookreme, and how grateful she was for all of the opportunities she'd been given. She talked about how, as an Asian American woman, she had hit many walls at other organizations, but at Brookreme she had been supported and encouraged.

The anecdotes were plentiful, and each person in the room lit up remembering special moments along the way they'd forgotten about. As Nancy listened, she also looked around the room at the faces of those listening in complete awe and enjoyment of their colleagues' masterful work. She recalled the times early in her career when she had dreamed of working in an environment like this instead of an oppressed sweatshop of obligated, self-serving people. She realized that Brookreme really had changed through this experience—in ways she hadn't expected.

About halfway through the stories, someone brought in appetizers and they were passed around. When the team had finished, the room broke into a rousing round of applause. Nancy got up and thanked each of them with the Brookreme soft high five and a hug, and they each made their way back to their seats. It was silent, but everyone knew Nancy had more to say. She took a deep breath and swallowed hard. It was clear that whatever she wanted to say wasn't easy for her.

"Look, you all know that I avoid PDE like the plague," she said, and the people surrounding her laughed warmly. "But just the same, it's hard not to be emotional in a moment like this. Listening to each of you talk about this process was utterly inspiring to me and, frankly, humbling. There's no way I could have done what you did, and I know it. When I think back to when I started at Brookreme, and how small and uncertain we were, and I see how far we've come, I'm amazed. Just amazed. For any of you who've been around awhile, you know what I'm talking about. And to be standing in Shanghai today, in Brookreme's offices here, where we will move onto the global stage as an organization, and to know that . . ." Nancy looked down at the floor, overcome with emotion, composed herself, and continued, "to know that each of you will be tomorrow's leaders of Brookreme—a Brookreme that is far different from the one we are leading today—well, I just don't have the words to tell you how grateful I am. I will be on the phone with the analysts in just a little while, and nothing will give me greater pleasure than to brag about each of you and what you've done. Every one of you had an important hand in getting us here and will have an important hand in seeing that we succeed here. And I know you will be every bit as exceptional as you've been so far. To every one of you, you have my deepest thanks. I'm proud to work with each one of you."

Again, the room broke into applause as Nancy walked back toward the conference room where she would talk by phone with the analyst community. Don walked out with her, and stopped just before they entered the conference room.

"I just want you to know, Nancy, that I know all of the heart and soul you've put into getting us here too," he said quietly. "That was incredibly generous of you to say all that you did back there. But I know how much you were doing behind the scenes to get us here too. You got us the resources, the board's support, the mobilization of Sydney and Chicago and California. *You* took the heat from people whose budgets were redirected to fund this. *You* dealt with the skeptics in the public and the media. And you kept your confidence strong even when you probably wanted to cut bait. So I want you to know that I'm grateful for you. I didn't want to say anything in there, because frankly, I didn't want to be seen as a suckup. Sure, it was a team effort and we all pulled through to get here. But your leadership, quieter though it might have been than the rest of ours, was every bit as vital to our success today, and I'm thankful for it. I noticed—even when it didn't seem like I did."

Nancy looked caught off guard. It had been a long time since someone had told her anything of the kind, and coming from Don, it especially meant a lot. All she could do was smile back at him and offer the Brookreme high five. But her smile lingered long enough to let Don know that what he said meant a lot. He knew he'd treaded twice today on her PDE aversion, and he privately felt proud of that.

The analyst call went swimmingly. Over the next couple of days, a variety of journal and media coverage acclaimed Brookreme's strategic advance. Nancy, Don, Sara, and Lana were all interviewed on several business talk radio shows, and on CNN's *Business Unusual*. There were parties in Chicago and Sydney in the weeks that followed as well.

About three weeks after the initial deal had been signed (and several others had been landed), Sara was back in Chicago packing up her office and apartment and getting ready to relocate to Shanghai. Nolan arranged a nice farewell luncheon for her. Many people stopped by to wish her well, and there were some fun gifts, including a staff picture that everyone signed for her, a beautiful book of photography of Shanghai that they also signed with good wishes, and some humorous gifts, like a copy of *China for Dummies*. Sara was flabbergasted at the graciousness of such a send-off. The success of Asia's launch had penetrated the organization to a degree none of the team could have expected. They'd been welcomed back like a World Series–winning baseball team returning to their home city.

As Sara finished labeling all of the boxes to be shipped and put the last items in the box she was taking home, Nancy stopped by. She hadn't been able to attend the luncheon that afternoon, but didn't want to miss the chance to wish Sara well.

"I can't believe I'm actually going through with this, Nancy." Sara shook her head in disbelief at the packed-up office.

"Well, it's a big step, kiddo," Nancy replied. "That's for sure. But you're ready for it. You've earned it."

"Thanks, Nancy," Sara said. "Not just for that, but for believing I could do this. For seeing past my quirks and giving me the chance for . . . for more. I promise, I won't let you down."

"Trust me, Sara, I'm not at all worried about you. I'm grateful you are willing to take on this assignment for Brookreme. We're off to a fabulous start, but keeping on that trajectory is another matter. I know you'll help us do that. So thank you."

"Well, you know I'll give this my all. It's going to be fun watching what Brookreme becomes in the next few years. I'm sure there's going to be more growing pains—we'll be more complex, have more products, and I guess becoming more sophisticated means the way we've always done things might not work. You see, I listened to you when you made that speech about change! Anyway, for now, I'm just gonna take this one day at a time. Thanks again, Nancy. Your support has meant more than you know."

"When can I expect that first call from you?" Nancy looked wryly at a perplexed Sara. "You said you'd be calling to talk to me—so, when can I expect your first call?"

"Oooh!" Sara got it, and laughed. "How about a month from today?"

"You're on. I'll look forward to it." Nancy marked the date in her PDA.

They walked out to the parking lot together, with the scantly lit Brookreme building as a backdrop, and a brisk Chicago chill in the air. They chatted a bit more about life in general. As Sara got to her car, she looked pensively at Nancy and said, "Today . . . today was a good day."

"They're all good, Sara. Even when they suck. Every day is a good day."

"I guess you're right, Nancy. It just depends on how you see it."

"Remember that when you get to Shanghai. You'll need it." With that, Nancy got into her car. She rolled down the window as she pulled out of her spot. "Go get 'em, kiddo, and I'll talk to you in a month. I want to hear all about all the good days you've had in between." Waving out the window, she drove off.

Sara gave one more glance back at the Brookreme building as she started her car. She had a funny feeling she'd be back here one day. She drove away, grateful for the good day she'd had, and hopeful for the good days ahead in the adventure that was about to unfold.

For the Moments Yet to Come . . .

1. For what are you grateful? How do you show it?

2. What is a good day for you? When the days are good, do you notice?

3. Does your community know they matter to you? In what ways could you better foster a sense of perpetual gratitude among them?

4. Do you have any new or different feelings about any of the characters at Brookreme now that you've been through the whole story?

EPILOGUE: BRIDGING THE DIVIDE

Go First to the Estuary

Something has changed within me
Something is not the same
I'm through with playing by the rules
Of someone else's game
Too late for second-guessing
Too late to go back to sleep
It's time to trust my instincts
Close my eyes, and leap!
It's time to try defying gravity . . .

Elpheba, "Defying Gravity," *Wicked*

I'm from New York—born and raised. Cynicism comes easy for me. Don't get me wrong, I love New York as passionately as anyone. And I wouldn't trade my heritage there for anything. But everyone knows that we Northeasterners come well equipped with a bit of a skeptical edge. Strangely, I'm also an idealist at heart. It's gotten me in trouble in my life, when I held out more optimism than circumstances realistically called for. Still, despite my New York roots, I do try and see half-full glasses before I see half-empty ones. Some days I can, and many days I don't.

Writing this book challenged the cynic in me. After more than two decades of working with organizations in a variety of ways, I have seen how ugly organizational life and leadership can get. I've grown weary of the quick-fix answers to leadership, as though leadership were no different from following a recipe to making a soufflé that doesn't fall in on itself, or following the directions to assemble one of those build-it-yourself pieces of furniture. Complex, yet doable if you follow the instructions.

Leadership, as you well know, is nothing of the sort. I am saddened every time I read of a leader whose lapsed judgment and greed has wounded hundreds of thousands of employees and shareholders. Such unnecessary destruction.

But despite such perverse distortions of leadership, I have great hope.

I still believe there are more good leaders than rotten ones. And certainly more leaders with the potential to become great leaders if given the chance. So researching and writing this material pushed some of my "yeah, right" buttons about how plausible these ideas are. I could hear in my head the voices of cynical leaders I've met, saying, "You've gotta be kidding me, Ron. You don't honestly expect people to try some of this stuff, do you? Nobody acts like that in the real world. Get a grip." But louder than the cynics were the voices of the men and women whose astounding stories grace these pages. They have marked me with good—and I hope they have marked you as well.

So yes, I do expect people to try harder, and I know many want to. And I'm glad to say people *do* act like this, more often than we might give them credit for. True, these aren't always the behaviors that get rewarded. But they are present. Sometimes they just need to be acknowledged, appreciated, and nurtured in the service of great communities and great performance.

For too long we've turned our heads and hearts away in avoidance of the messiness of leadership relationships. And we are paying a price for that. The next generation of leaders is opting out. And this generation of leaders is writing them off. I don't know about you, but this grieves me to watch. Because there is so much talent and goodness in both.

If you are more realist than idealist, ask yourself this hard question: What are those with whom you lead saying about you when they sit at the dinner table with their families? Because rest assured, if the stories they tell in the evening of their day with you are distasteful, you can bet the performance you get the next day will be too.

There's a research study done a number of years ago that I believe says a great deal. It was a study among baseball umpires. The research premise was to determine how it is that umpires could make quick calls with such a clear degree of certainty. The first umpire answered, "Well, that's easy. If it's a ball, I call it a ball; if it's a strike, I call it a strike." The second umpire said, "I just call 'em the way I see 'em." Clearly these first two umpires were suggesting that well-grooved intuition and years of experience were the primary factors in their ability. The third umpire said something profound. He said, "Well, it's really simple. Because they ain't nothin' until I call 'em."

And that's true with life.

Life isn't anything until you call it. So if you want to call your leadership and your organization "as good as it gets," then you'll be right, and you'll have no more than what you have now. But if you want to call your leadership and your organization "more than meets the eye," then you also will be right, and you will see leaders around you rise up to join you. And they will see you as one with whom they will be grateful to lead.

What will you choose to see on your leadership horizon? Are you willing to strain to see beyond what is common? Will you work against even your own cynicism about what it is possible to achieve in your organization? As a leader? As a human being?

Remaining divided from others, especially those different from you, is frankly easy. You get to complain and be right. And in safety, you are free from having to change. But that safety has a substantial cost. You could be mortgaging the future of your organization. If you can suspend your belief about what *is* long enough to imagine what *could be*, you could bridge a divide that unleashes a future for leaders yet to be. You have to be willing to let the saltwater and freshwater come together. You have to let your voice, and the voices of others, flow together in an estuary of sorts—where a unique habitat is formed that gives rise to unimaginable performance. In an increasingly global environment, where traditional boundaries and borders are blurring by the day, where horizontal structures of collaboration are replacing vertical structures of hierarchy at unprecedented speeds, where once-unassailable competitive advantages are being commoditized, the only differentiating element a leader can bring to bear is the power of strong, mutually beneficial relationships.

If your eyes have been so preconditioned that you can't—or won't—allow yourself to see beyond what is, then I am sad for you. If the sound of your voice blended with the voices of many leaders is unappealing, then you are forfeiting more than you realize.

But if you have even a shred of hope, an ounce of desire for more, then stoke that appetite with all your might, and reach for the greatest leadership imaginable—by reaching for others. And allow them to reach back toward you. And when you can acknowledge that others have imprinted you with their very best and have invited you to return the favor, you will know you are leading well.

To lead well, you must choose relationship.

Will you go first?
And what will you choose to see?

> *A philosopher once wrote you need three things to have a good life: one, a meaningful relationship; two, a decent job of work; and three, to make a difference. And it was always that third one that stressed me, to make a difference. And I realize that I do. Every day, we all do. It's how we interact, with our fellow man.*
> *[Interviewer: "How would you like to be remembered?"]*
> *Simply, as the man who put a smile on the face of all who he met.*
>
> DAVID BRENT, *regional manager* WERNHAM HOGG
> *The Office*

REFERENCES AND RESOURCES

Allender, D. B. *Leading with a Limp: Turning Your Struggles into Strengths.* Colorado Springs, Colo.: WaterBrook Press, 2006.

Berglas, S. "The Very Real Dangers of Executive Coaching." *Harvard Business Review,* June 2002.

Block, P. *Stewardship: Choosing Service Over Self-Interest.* San Francisco: Berrett-Koehler, 1996.

Bracken, D. W., Timmreck, C. W., and Church, A. H. (eds.). *The Handbook of Multisource Feedback.* Hoboken, N.J.: Wiley, 2000.

Brown, J., and Isaacs, D. *The World Café: Shaping Our Futures Through Conversations That Matter.* San Francisco: Berrett-Koehler, 2005.

Byrnes, N., Byrne, J. A., Edwards, C., Lee, L., Holmes, S., and Muller, J. "James Sinegal, Costco: The Bargain Hunter." *Business Week,* September 23, 2002.

Chaleff, I. *The Courageous Follower: Standing Up To and For Our Leaders.* San Francisco: Berrett-Koehler, 2002.

Corporate Executive Board, Corporate Leadership Council. *Realizing the Full Potential of Rising Talent, Volume I.* Washington, D.C.: Corporate Executive Board, 2005.

Dauten, D. A. *The Gifted Boss: How to Find, Create, and Keep Great Employees.* New York: Morrow, 1999.

Deming, W. E. *Out of the Crisis.* Boston: MIT Press, 1986.

Dillard, A. *Pilgrim at Tinker Creek.* New York: HarperCollins, 1998.

Drake Beam Morin, Inc. "DBM Survey Finds Companies Have Not Prepared Younger Workers for Senior Leadership Roles." *DBM Press Release #14,* July 14, 2003.

French, J.R.P., and Raven, B. H. "The Bases of Social Power." In D. Cartwright (ed.), *Studies in Social Power.* Ann Arbor, Mich.: Institute for Social Research, 1959.

Haugen, G. A., and Hunter, G. *Terrify No More: Young Girls Held Captive and the Daring Undercover Operation to Win Their Freedom.* Nashville, Tenn.: W Publishing Group, 2005.

Katcher, B. L. "How to Improve Employee Trust in Management." Discovery Surveys, www.discoverysurveys.com/articles/itw-019.html.

"Leadership Survey on Pastors and Internet Pornography." *Leadership,* Winter, 2001.

Lencioni, P. *Death by Meeting: A Leadership Fable about Solving the Most Painful Problem in Business.* Hoboken, N.J.: Wiley, 2004.

Marshall, E. M. *Building Trust at the Speed of Change: The Power of the Relationship-Based Corporation.* New York: AMACOM, 1999.

Martinez, M. "Blockbuster Drugs Go Generic." *Puerto Rico Herald,* June 19, 2003.

McClintock, J. "Leadership Development Crisis Looms as Boomers Retire, Firm Reports." *San Gabriel Valley Tribune,* July 17, 2003.

McGinnis, M. L. *Bringing Out the Best in People: How to Enjoy Helping Others Excel.* Minneapolis, Minn.: Augsburg Fortress, 1985.

Naik, G. "GlaxoSmithKline Actively Pursues Drug Licenses." *The Wall Street Journal,* February 13, 2002.

Nielsen, J. S. *The Myth of Leadership: Creating Leaderless Organizations.* Mountain View, Calif.: Consulting Psychologists Press, 2004.

Perlow, L., and Williams, S. "Is Silence Killing Your Company?" *Harvard Business Review,* May 2003.

Pollard, C. W. *The Soul of the Firm.* Grand Rapids, Mich.: Zondervan, 1996.

Power, S., and Karnitschnig, M. "VW's Woes Mount Amid Claims of Sex Junkets for Union Chiefs." *The Wall Street Journal,* November 17, 2005.

Shaffer, C. R., and Anundsen, K. *Creating Community Anywhere.* New York: Penguin, 1993.

Simmons, A. *A Safe Place for Dangerous Truths: Using Dialogue to Overcome Fear and Distrust at Work.* New York: AMACOM, 1999.

Simon, E. "How to Make Investors Whole?" *Philadelphia Inquirer,* January 29, 2006.

Tichy, N. M., and Cohen, E. B. *The Leadership Engine: How Winning Companies Build Leaders at Every Level.* New York: HarperCollins, 2002.

University of Michigan, ANES. American National Election Studies: 1964–1996. Ann Arbor: University of Michigan, 1958–1996.

Von Oech, R. *A Whack on the Side of the Head.* New York: Time Warner, 1998.

Wheatley, M. J. *Finding Our Way: Leadership in an Uncertain Time.* San Francisco: Berrett-Koehler, 2005.

Zander, R. S., and Zander, B. *The Art of Possibility: Transforming Professional and Personal Life.* Boston: Harvard Business School Publishing, 2000.

ACKNOWLEDGMENTS

Two years ago, when I started this project, I could never have imagined how much of an adventure—and how much fun—it would turn out to be. As I wrote these pages, I was passing through one of the greatest crucibles of my life, making the transition from one coast to another, uprooting my family and disrupting my entire life to forge new chapters. Both the joy and the struggle of those years are in these pages.

Goethe said, "At the moment of commitment, the universe conspires to assist you." It certainly felt like the universe came out in full force to bring this book to life. Only with the gracious talents and support of these friends and colleagues was it a miracle waiting to happen. Each of you has been a champion to me, and I am grateful.

Neal Maillet and *Susan Williams* at Jossey-Bass, for staying in the conversation long enough and for pushing my thinking far enough for us all to catch the vision. Many thanks.

Michael Russell and *Zach Brittle,* for your creative, editorial, and research brilliance. A more stunning team I could never have asked for. Thanks for diving into the deep end of the pool with belief. Your fingerprints run deep in these pages. I have been fortunate to watch and learn from your artistry. You are gentlemen and scholars. And to *Andrew Ballard* at Marketing Solutions, I'm grateful for your tenacious skill to penetrate any organization on the planet and extract limitless data. You are masterful.

Mindy Millward and *Ulrich Nettesheim,* my Passages Consulting colleagues, how did I ever get so blessed to have comrades, colleagues, and friends like the two of you? Thanks for helping me fall in love all over again with the noble work of leadership and organizational transformation. Alongside the two of you, what could be better?

Mike Roberts, Dr. Beth Seidenberg, Gary Haugen, and your respective colleagues, and the many CEOs and executives who spoke with us, for your inspiring and insightful stories, which will undoubtedly reach many. I'm privileged to know you and to have learned from you. You are incomparable leaders.

Tim Soerens, Joel VandenBrink, Tom Ryan, Bob Saracen, and *Mindy* and *Ulrich,* for reading chapter by chapter and offering great insights and ideas. And a special thanks to Tim, for providing so much encouraging inspiration for me to stick with this, and for that auspicious email urging me to "click Send." You are optimism in motion. *Josh Epperson,* a phenomenal job on the final proof. Your future as an agent of major change is brighter than you imagine. Your partnership is a gift.

Ronna Miller and the *Mars Hill Graduate School Leadership Crucible team, Paul Steinke, Zach, Jason Best, Crystal Miller, Josh, Meredith Dancause, Steve Dancause, Tim, Joel, J. Paul Fridenmaker, Jon DeWaal, Cathy Loerzel, Haley Clark, Jen Grabarczyk, Josh Reynolds, Josh Sandoz, Josue Blanco, Selena Gray, Abby Long, Tom, Dan Allender,* and *Lisa Philabaum.* Thank you ever so much for allowing me such a grand experiment, and for your courageous and passionate leadership of an extraordinary event. Without it, this book could never have been born. Each of you is an exemplary leader. I have no doubt you will change whatever part of the world you find yourself in. Consider these chapters *your* story. Ronna, a special thanks for adding the "dares" and your kind friendship to me. You are an elegant and gifted leader. Paul, you are gourmet food to my soul. Crystal, Meredith, Josh E., Steve, Tim, Joel, Jon, Tom, Cathy, Haley, Jen, Josh R., Josue, Selena, Josh S., Abby—what school wouldn't be brimming with pride and delight to have students like you? Look out planet, 'cause you people are goin' places! J. Paul—your picture is in the dictionary next to *servant leadership.* You are a gift. Jason, your media and technology talents are astounding. Please remember us all in your Academy Award acceptance speech. Dan, I would never want to be in this strange game without you. That our paths have crossed with such force only tells me God has a sense of humor and that there is much to be done between us, by us, and for us. Thank you for inviting me into your world. Lisa—without you, I would have no life. Your friendship and comradeship keep me going more than you can know.

Cathy Martin—thank you for teaching me about estuaries. You're a gifted and insightful executive.

Mike McCoy—your kindness, generosity, perseverance, and wisdom are a gift.

Jim, Rich, Bob, Steven, and *Wes*—my personal "band of brothers." Doing life with each of you makes life worth it and an adventure extraordinaire. Though we are scattered to the corners of the earth, each of you is never far from me.

And to *Barbara, Matthew,* and *Rebecca*—your love and support are the fuel in my soul. For sacrificing the time to allow me to complete this, and for your unending love and joy, no man could ask for a family to journey life with as wonderful as you. I love you.

And to *my God,* for loving, tolerating, surprising, and stretching me, all as you promised. My love and devotion are yours. Small crumbs, yet all I have.

Ron Carucci

The Author

RON CARUCCI is a seasoned consultant with more than twenty years of experience working with leaders of organizations ranging from the Fortune 50 to start-ups in pursuit of transformational change. He is a founding partner with Passages Consulting, LLC (www.passagesconsulting.com). Ron works in the areas of large-scale organization and culture change, enterprise organization architecture design, CEO development, executive leadership and selection, and building executive teams, as well as strategy formulation and implementation. Passages Consulting also specializes in the creation of high-impact executive leadership development processes through the combined use of simulations, action learning, and personal development strategies. Prior to launching Passages Consulting with his colleagues, he was a managing partner at the acclaimed Delta Consulting, LLC.

Ron also serves as chief operating officer and professor of leadership at Mars Hill Graduate School in Seattle, Washington. He has a passion to see emerging leaders find their voice and thrive in the process of preparing to lead in the future. As part of Mars Hill Conferences, he co-led the creation of *The Leadership Crucible,* a powerful leadership tool whereby leaders immerse themselves in a fictitious city and assume the roles of executive members of organizations in that city (www.leadershipcrucible.com).

Most recently, Ron has been working with CEOs of both large enterprises and start-up organizations on the challenges of managing growth. He has helped organizations re-architect themselves for global scale-up, devise turnaround strategies, and build appropriate talent strategies to ensure the effective selection, development, retention, and reward of key leaders of major growth businesses.

Ron is a faculty member at Fordham University Graduate School, serving as an associate professor of organizational behavior.

His clients have included Novartis, Bristol-Myers Squibb, Amgen, McDonald's, Gates, RehabCare, Phase 2 Consulting, PepsiCo, ADP, Edward Jones Investments, Citigroup, OhioHealth, Deutsche Bank, PricewaterhouseCoopers, Accenture, Corning Inc., World Kitchen, Business for Social Responsibility, TIAA-CREF, and Raytheon. Ron is a frequent speaker at national and international conferences on leadership and organizational transformation.

He is coauthor of the book *The Value Creating Consultant: How to Build and Sustain Lasting Client Relationships* (AMACOM, 2000) as well as the book *Relationships That Enable Enterprise Change* (Jossey-Bass, 2002). He has also authored numerous articles and book chapters on the issues of organizational change and forming effective trusted advisor relationships.

Visit Ron at: